The Ranger's Guide to YELLOWSTONE

Insider Advice from Ranger Norm

by
Susan and Phil Frank

AVALON TRAVEL

The Ranger's Guide to Yellowstone
1st Edition

Avalon Travel
a member of the Perseus Books Group
1700 Fourth Street
Berkeley, CA 94710, USA
atpfeedback@avalonpub.com
www.avalontravelbooks.com

Editors: Grace Fujimoto, Michelle Cadden
Graphics Coordinator: Stefano Boni
Production Coordinator: Darren Alessi
Cover Designer: Darren Alessi
Indexer: Judy Hunt

ISBN-10: 1-59880-127-9
ISBN-13: 978-1-59880-127-9
ISSN: 1941-8485

Printing History
1st Edition — July 2008
5 4 3 2 1

Printed in the United States by RR Donnelley

Contents

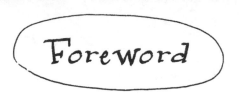

Foreword

Yellowstone is many things to many people. To me, for seventeen years, it was home.

I loved looking at the elk, bison, grizzly bears, wolves, and wildflowers of the alpine tundra and montane meadows. I enjoyed listening to the wind across Swan Lake Flat, the waves on the shore of Yellowstone Lake, the howls of coyotes—and, more recently, wolves. I took in the smells of rain and lupine; of sagebrush bruised by running elk; the rotten-egg smell of hydrogen sulfide wafting from the thermal areas (though I never quite got used to that). I remember turning so that the winter sun would thaw my face in zero-degree weather. Hiking the trails and canoeing the lakes made summer and fall memorable.

Yellowstone remains fascinating to me because people keep discovering surprising new things about it. They keep learning that Yellowstone is chaotic, complex, and catastrophic. Everything keeps changing, sometimes very suddenly and at a scale that is truly awesome.

Yellowstone's crust keeps deforming—inflating and deflating—like the body of a sleeping animal. Geologists say there is enough heat for future cataclysmic events, although they can't say when. The heat flow in the Yellowstone thermal areas is nearly twenty times the continental average, and it powers all the geothermal features that make Yellowstone unique.

In 1995, we released 14 gray wolves from Canada in Yellowstone; in 1996, another 17. As of December 2007, there were 171 wolves in 11 packs in the park. After more than 50 years' absence, wolves have resumed their role in the interactions of myriad creatures and plants in the park, enhancing biological diversity.

Yellowstone is a place distinctly rich in wildlife; now that the wolves are back, it's also the only ecosystem in the contiguous United States that contains every species that was native to the area when Europeans came to the Americas. As such, it has inestimable value as a place where we can learn how intact ecosystems work. All the forces—geological, climatic, and biological—operate here. They are not benign forces; the volcanic explosions that took place millions of years ago undoubtedly wiped out all life over thousands of square miles and changed the climate of the earth. The widespread wildfires of the 1870s and 1988 changed the face of the landscape. The drought of the 1920s and 1930s drastically reduced the extent of willow communities in low-lying valleys. Some combination of factors in the late 1870s allowed aspen clones to produce large trees that are dying now and not being replaced—no one really knows why.

If I've learned anything in my 17 years in Yellowstone, it is that nothing is simple. All the elements are interconnected and interactive. For centuries, scholars have been considering the concept of balance in nature. What is demonstrated in natural systems, exemplified by Yellowstone, is instead chaos, complexity, catastrophe, and certainly surprise. I've also learned that a human lifetime is a poor scale for measuring significant events in a place like Yellowstone.

Looking for something and being pleasantly surprised to find something else even more valuable is serendipity. I came to Yellowstone seeking to advance my career. I left Yellowstone with a sense of belonging there. If you as a visitor to the park can sense, even for a few hours or days, the majesty of Yellowstone's vast landscape, if you can feel the beauty and dignity of its plants and wildlife, if you can begin to grasp the immensity and complexity of the place, then you are on your way to a lifetime of discovery. If this little book can speed you on your way, I'm glad.

Norm Bishop
Bozeman, Montana

Introduction

Visiting Yellowstone, you can easily be overwhelmed by the wealth of natural wonders, activities, accommodations, and facilities arrayed before you. You'll probably want to ask a few questions to figure out what to do when and how. This book is meant to offer you a quick and easy way of finding the answers you need. Your guide in these pages will be Ranger Norm, a fictional character based loosely on Norm Bishop, a veteran ranger who was at Yellowstone long enough to have heard all the questions that visitors ask—and to know the answers. We thought he would be a natural to guide you through the park as only an insider can.

The question-and-answer format we use originally came from "100+ Common Visitor Questions & Answers" (revised April 1995), a document by the National Park Service Division of Interpretation at Yosemite National Park created to help park rangers and interpretive staff there get oriented quickly.

We've updated many of those questions, provided answers specific to Yellowstone, and added lots of others to help you learn some insider information about this magnificent park and its surroundings. We hope the book will add to your enjoyment of Yellowstone, whatever your interests and however long your visit.

Acknowledgments

We are indebted to Norm Bishop and Josh Englander for their invaluable help in developing and editing the manuscript; Lee H. Whittlesey for his review of the manuscript, and research librarians Kathryn Lancaster and Barbara Zafft of the Yellowstone Center for Resources for their generous assistance with research and resource materials; Pat Cole, Jeff Brown and the Yellowstone Association for their review of the manuscript; Dr. John E. McCosker of the California Academy of Sciences for his technical review and expertise; Dennis Glick and the Greater Yellowstone Coalition for their help with research materials; Doug Wachob, Sharon Guenther, Diane Carillo, and the Teton Science School; John Greve and Carrie Ward of Hamilton Stores; retired NPS Ranger Chet Harris for his careful review of the manuscript; and the National Park Service staff at Yellowstone—especially Doug Smith, Amanda Hardy, Stacy Churchwell, Karen Angerman, Gregg Kurz, Dan Nazone, Leslie Wiedeman, and Jennifer Whipple—for their help in making this guidebook as accurate as possible. Thanks also to Janet Deun, Judy den Boer, Stacy Frank, and Pam McCosker for their help in researching and producing the information.

We would like to thank Grace Fujimoto of Avalon Travel for her help in making this new edition possible. And for their invaluable help in updating the information for the new edition, we wish to thank Ranger Ivan Kowski, as well as Lorrie Gallagher, Alice Rogers, Pam McCosker, and Lynne Sanditen. We would also like to thank Norm Bishop once again for his invaluable contributions to the new edition.

S. F. and P. F.

1.
Getting
There

YELLOWSTONE
NATIONAL PARK
·JUST AHEAD·

Where is Yellowstone?

A volcanic landscape filled with steaming geysers, plentiful wildlife, petrified forests, and vast canyons and valleys, Yellowstone National Park spills over the northwest corner of Wyoming and just into Montana and Idaho. The park spreads over 2.2 million acres (3,400 square miles) of high-elevation forests, sharp mountains, and semiarid plains, straddling the continental divide. It's home to the headwaters of three great rivers—the Yellowstone, the Madison, and the Snake. And it's the heart of the Greater Yellowstone Ecosystem, 18 million acres that include Yellowstone and Grand Teton National Parks, seven national forests, many designated wilderness areas, and three wildlife refuges. This ecosystem is home to a fascinating array of wild animals, plants, and geological wonders.

Here are some road mileage figures and approximate driving times to Yellowstone (based on 50 miles per hour outside the park and 45 miles per hour inside the park):

Via Highway 89 from the north:

Gardiner, Montana	0 miles
Livingston, Montana	52 miles (1 hour)
Bozeman, Montana	75 miles (1.5 hours)
Seattle, Washington	800 miles (16 hours)

Via Highway 89 from the south:

Jackson, Wyoming	56 miles (1.25 hours)
Salt Lake City, Utah	390 miles (8 hours)
Denver, Colorado	563 miles (11.5 hours)

Via Highway 20 from the west:

West Yellowstone, Montana	0.3 miles
Ashton, Idaho	63 miles (1.25 hours)
Idaho Falls, Idaho	116 miles (2.5 hours)
Las Vegas, Nevada	809 miles (16 hours)
San Francisco, California	1,061 miles (22 hours)

Via Highway 212 from the northeast:

Silver Gate, Montana	1 mile
Cooke City, Montana	3 miles
Red Lodge, Montana	69 miles (1.5 hours)
Billings, Montana	125 miles (2.5 hours)

Via Highway 16 from the east:

Cody, Wyoming	53 miles (1 hour)
Buffalo, Wyoming	235 miles (5 hours)
Rapid City, South Dakota	460 miles (9.5 hours)
Omaha, Nebraska	946 miles (20 hours)

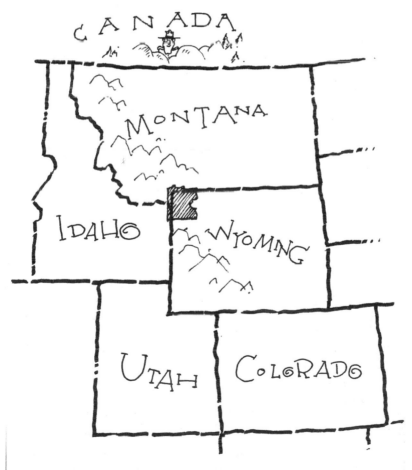

What is the Greater Yellowstone Ecosystem?

Yellowstone's 2.2 million acres are just a small part of what scientists call an *ecosystem*—an area where animals, plants, minerals, water, and climate work together in a dynamic way, as a system. The Greater Yellowstone Ecosystem includes Grand Teton National Park, seven national forests, many designated wilderness areas, three wildlife refuges, and parts of three states. We rangers see our ecosystem as a very large interconnected whole that doesn't separate Yellowstone or Grand Teton National Park from the surrounding wilderness areas or wildlife refuges. If we could take away all the boundaries set by humans and put everything together, we'd have nearly 18 million acres of an interactive system that includes a unique landscape, wild animals, and plants, all of which depend upon one another to stay alive—plus around 220,000 of us human residents who love it.

The Greater Yellowstone Area may be the largest intact ecosystem in the temperate region of the earth. Many animals that call this ecosystem home— grizzly bears, swans, bison, elk, and others—migrate through the various areas according to where the food is and what the season is. Which means we have a dynamic place, in which the animals are constantly moving. The same is true of plants, although they "travel" more slowly through the ecosystem, as they're carried by animals or weather over longer periods of time. The animals and plants evolved together, so they can survive despite the harshness of the winters. But boundaries created by people complicate the lives of the migratory animals.

For the visitor, Greater Yellowstone means 18 million acres of wildland opportunities—a place where you can pitch a tent, toss a line in a stream that's part of a major river system of the western United States, view some of the country's most beautiful wildlife, carry a boat to one of hundreds of lakes, or enjoy many other outdoor activities. As I guide you through this beautiful park, I'll also give you tips on exploring beyond Yellowstone and inside the Greater Yellowstone Ecosystem.

For more information on this ecosystem, contact Greater Yellowstone Coordinating Committee (406/522-8575, http://bsi.montana.edu/web/gycc/home), the Greater Yellowstone Area Team Leader Office (P.O. Box 2556, Billings, MT

59103), or the Greater Yellowstone Coalition (P.O. Box 1874, Bozeman, MT 59771, 406/586-1593 or 800/775-1834, www.greateryellowstone.org).

Here's what's included in the Greater Yellowstone Area:

National Forests (62 percent)
Bridger-Teton National Forest
Shoshone National Forest
Custer National Forest
Gallatin National Forest
Beaverhead National Forest
Targhee National Forest
Caribou National Forest

Bureau of Land Management Lands (less than 10 percent)

Indian Reservations (2 percent)
Wind River Indian Reservation

State-Owned Lands (2 percent)

National Wildlife Refuges (0.5 percent)
Red Rock Lakes National
    Wildlife Refuge
Grays Lake National
    Wildlife Refuge
National Elk Refuge

Privately Owned Lands (19 percent)

National Parks (14 percent)
Yellowstone National Park
Grand Teton National Park

How do we get there?

Depending upon your time and budget, you can get to Yellowstone by car, plane, or bus. There's no direct train service to the park.

By Car

There are several entrances to the park. From the south, you enter from Dubois or Jackson, Wyoming, via Grand Teton National Park and Rockefeller Memorial Parkway, then follow the Lewis River Canyon past Moose Falls and Lewis Lake all the way to Grant Village with its visitor center and the West Thumb Geyser Basin along Yellowstone Lake.

The north approach follows the Yellowstone River from Livingston, Montana, through Paradise Valley and Gardiner, Montana, where you'll drive through the Theodore Roosevelt Entrance Arch to Mammoth Hot Springs,

Old Fort Yellowstone, and the Albright Visitor Center.

The most frequently used approach is from the west, through Idaho and Montana via Highway 20, taking you through the Targhee National Forest to West Yellowstone, into the park, then along the Madison River, which winds through Madison Canyon. Here you'll find National Park Mountain, where an early exploration team camped in 1870.

You approach the northeast entrance from Red Lodge, Montana, over the winding but scenic Beartooth Highway in the Absaroka Mountain Range to Cooke City, Montana. A dip down through Icebox Canyon opens to the Lamar Valley with its fossil forest, elk and bison herds, and wolf packs. Another spectacular approach, which goes from Cody, Wyoming, to Cooke City, Montana, is the steep and winding Chief Joseph Memorial Highway.

From Cody, Wyoming, you follow Highway 212 along the North Fork of the

Shoshone River and cross the Absaroka Range at Sylvan Pass (elevation 8,541 feet) inside the park's east entrance.

In the winter, the north entrance through Gardiner, Montana, which dead-ends at Cooke City, Montana, is the only one open to automobile traffic. The west, south, and east entrances are accessible only to over-snow vehicles. Call 307/344-7381 for current road conditions and information.

By Plane

You can fly to the following airports to visit Yellowstone: Billings, Montana (129 miles to north entrance); Bozeman, Montana (75 miles to north entrance); West Yellowstone, Montana (three miles to west entrance, summer only); Jackson Hole, Wyoming (50 miles to south entrance), and Cody, Wyoming (53 miles to east entrance). Rental cars are available at the airports and in major towns near the park.

By Bus

Greyhound Bus Lines (800/231-2222, www.greyhound.com) take you to Bozeman and Livingston, Montana, where you can get connecting service to West Yellowstone, Montana, or can rent a car and drive through the north entrance at Gardiner, Montana. Gray Line Bus Tours (800/443-6133, www

.grayline.com) serve Jackson Hole, Wyoming, with connecting service into the park. Gray Line buses only run seasonally, so call ahead for information. For a list of operators, look under "Transportation" in the *Licensed Tour Operators and Outfitters* section of the *Quick Reference* chapter.

Special Tours

Plenty of commercial companies offer tours to Yellowstone. Check the list in the *Licensed Tour Operators and Outfitters* section of the *Quick Reference* chapter, or call your travel agent.

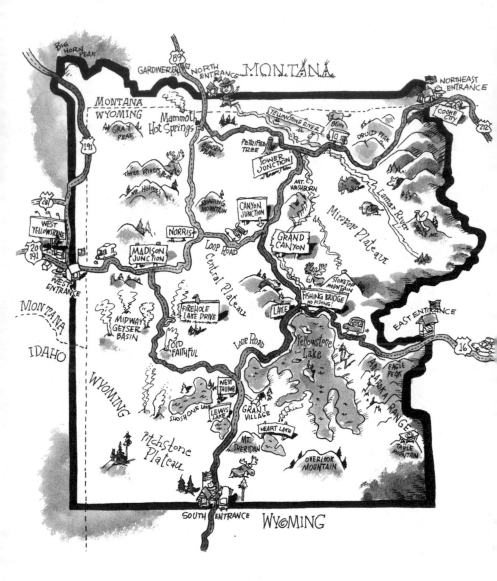

Is the park always open to visitors?

The park is supposed to be open 24 hours a day, 365 days a year, but we've learned not to fool with Mother Nature. In 1988, a dozen major fires roared through the park, closing some roads for part of the summer. Another fire in 1994 had similar effects. An earthquake rattled us in 1959, causing closures of certain areas while rangers determined the extent of the damage and potential hazards to visitors. Snow can close park roads any day of the year.

We close all park entrances for a month and a half on the first Sunday of November, to get the park ready for the big snows. (You can still ski or hike in.) Around the middle of December, depending on the weather, we open the north and northeast entrances to automobile traffic and the west, south, and east entrances to over-snow vehicles only, for the winter season. When the spring thaw begins, usually in the third week of March, we close all entrances again for a month to prepare for the spring and summer seasons. In mid-April, we reopen all entrances to visitors in cars and buses. We call the closure periods our "shoulder seasons." They help the staff prepare the park and its facilities for seasonal changes in temperature, weather, and numbers of visitors.

Call 307/344-7381 for 24-hour information on park and road conditions.

What's the best time of the year to see Yellowstone?

Speaking from experience I can say that any season in Yellowstone has its rewards. It just depends on what you want to see and do.

Spring conditions usually arrive around the beginning of May. The backcountry trails are closed by 2–3 feet of snow, but visitors can still enjoy the awesome sights of rivers swollen with runoff, waterfalls in full bloom, and meadows turned to lakes of snowmelt. With the lower elevations clear of snow, we open the roads into the park, but hiking our trails can be a pretty muddy experience. Our spring weather is unpredictable, with days of rain, some snow, and daytime temperatures ranging 45–65°F, dropping to 10–30°F in the evenings. Toward the end of May or early June, if you drive, especially in the Madison-Firehole, Lamar, and Hayden Valleys, you're sure to see brick-red baby bison, newborn elk, and an occasional grizzly fresh out of winter hibernation.

Summer hits with a bang around July 4 and usually ends about two months later. This is the park's "high" season, when most of the year's visitors come to see wildlife, thermal features, and waterfalls, take pictures of it all, and hike. A few fish the lakes and streams and use boats on the big lakes. Only the very hardy swim, because the water is very cold. Air temperatures range 60–75°F during the day, 25–40°F at night. On most days, the number of cars on park roads averages in the thousands.

During the fall, Yellowstone lives up to its colorful name. Aspen trees turn gold, and grassy valleys turn various shades of bronze. Many of us who live here year-round consider this time—mid-September–early November— the best: warm, bright days with temperatures between 40 and 55°F and crisp, frosty nights ranging 15–35°F. It's the season when our wildlife begins to

PUTT
PUTT
PUTT
PUTT
PUTT
PUTT
UTT

congregate at the lower elevations. Bull elk and moose and buck deer have polished their antlers for the mating season, and the sound of elk bugling is everywhere. Anglers find that lower water levels in the streams make fishing conditions prime.

We get an occasional snowstorm in October, but winter really comes in November. Then big storms transform the park into a vast snowscape dotted with steaming geysers and hot springs. Although winter has its own beauty, it's not an easy time for park wildlife. Often, they have to make a life-or-death decision either to leave the park for snow-free grazing or to stay close to warm thermal areas, lower valleys, or wind-blown ridgetops, where they must constantly paw through deep snow to reach the abundant forage underneath. Snowmobiles and over-snow vehicles called snow-coaches replace automobiles on most of the park roads mid-December–mid-March, and we snowshoe or ski to enjoy our backcountry areas.

It's a real bargain, considering that you're paying to see some of the most beautiful and dynamic scenery in the country and one of the world's greatest wildlife refuges.

As you enter one of five park gates, you'll pay an entrance fee that's good for seven days for both Yellowstone *and* Grand Teton National Park. A ranger will give you a map of the park with basic park information, an admission receipt, and a free copy of *Yellowstone Today*—the park newspaper, which gives up-to-date listings and schedules for all park activities. One can access the online version of *Yellowstone Today* via the Yellowstone National Park website (www.nps.gov/yell/planyourvisit/yellowstone-today.htm). Remember to keep your admission receipt to reenter either park. For educational fee waivers, call 307/344-2107.

Private noncommercial vehicles. $25
(valid for seven days, both parks)

Individuals arriving by motorcycle or snowmobile $20
(valid for seven days, both parks)

Individuals arriving by bus, foot, bicycle, horse, or skis $12
(valid for seven days, both parks)

Annual Pass $50
(valid for one year from date of purchase for both parks)

America the Beautiful—Annual Pass $80
(good for all national parks for one year from date of purchase)

America the Beautiful—Senior Pass $10
(lifetime pass to all national parks for U.S. citizens
or permanent residents who are 62 and older)

America the Beautiful—Access Pass. . . . . .Free
(pass for blind or permanently disabled U.S. citizens or permanent residents)

What services are available?

Yellowstone National Park is so varied and vast that visitors may have a hard time taking it all in. To make it easier, we divide the park into five areas, each with one or more small centers with varying services for visitors. The good news is, the centers are never more than 22 miles apart. Here are the centers and their services:

Old Faithful Temporary Visitor Center
Old Faithful Visitor Center, Yellowstone Association Bookstore, three Yellowstone General Stores, Old Faithful Inn, Old Faithful Lodge Cabins, gift stores, Old Faithful Snow Lodge and Cabins, food services (ranging from an informal snack shop to full-service dining rooms), service stations, post office, ATM, ranger station and medical clinic, and snow-coach touring. A new visitor education center at Old Faithful will open in 2011.

Grant Village
Grant Visitor Center, hotel, Yellowstone Association Bookstore, Yellowstone General Store, food service, mini-store, auto towing and repair, service station, campground, boat ramp, ranger station, amphitheater, self-service laundry, public showers, sanitary dump station.

West Thumb Information Station
Hydrothermal interpretive display and boardwalk, Yellowstone Association Bookstore, parking, public restrooms.

Bridge Bay
Ranger station, boat marina, campground, Yellowstone Marina Store, boat ramp, boat rentals, boat tours, amphitheater, sanitary dump station.

Lake Hotel and Lodge
Lake Yellowstone Hotel and Cabins, Lake Lodge and Cabins, Yellowstone Association Bookstore, Yellowstone General Store, gift store, ATM, range of food services, ranger station, hospital.

Fishing Bridge
Fishing Bridge Visitor Center, ranger station, RV park with full hookups, Yellowstone General Store, food service, service station, auto towing and repair, self-service laundry, public showers, sightseeing tours, amphitheater, sanitary dump station.

Canyon Village

Canyon Visitor Education Center, Yellowstone Association Bookstore, ranger station, Canyon Lodge and Cabins, post office, Yellowstone General Store, gift store, food service, Nature Shop, ATM, campground, auto towing and repair, self-service laundry, public showers, saddle horses, amphitheater, sanitary dump station.

Tower Falls

Campground, Yellowstone General Store, snack service.

Tower Junction and Roosevelt Lodge

Ranger station, Roosevelt Lodge Cabins, Yellowstone General Store, gift store, food service, saddle horses, stagecoach rides, cookouts, service station.

Mammoth Hot Springs

Park Headquarters and Albright Visitor Center, Yellowstone Association Bookstore, Mammoth Hot Springs Hotel and Cabins, range of food services, gift store, Yellowstone General Store, Nature Shop, campground, service station, post office, saddle horses, medical clinic, snow-coach touring.

Norris

National Park Service Ranger Museum, Yellowstone Association Bookstore, campground, snack service.

Madison Area

Museum, Yellowstone Association Bookstore, campground, amphitheater, sanitary dump station.

Who runs Yellowstone?

Although the park belongs to all of us, the National Park Service (NPS), which is part of the U.S. Department of the Interior, makes the rules to protect resources and people in Yellowstone National Park. This means you won't see any highway patrol officers, sheriffs, or municipal firefighters during your visit. Look instead for one of us park rangers if you need a helping hand.

The NPS has plenty of people who make sure things run smoothly. Park rangers handle law enforcement, traffic regulation, search and rescue, and other duties. Park naturalists and interpreters provide all the educational walks, talks, and programs in the park. The people dressed in green pants, gray shirts, and dark green baseball caps may be rangers, interpreters, or the park maintenance, fire, and resource management workers. All of us report to NPS managers such as the superintendent and chief ranger.

The Yellowstone Association (YA) provides informational and interpretive publications in support of park programs and provides funds for exhibits, preservation of historic park buildings and artifacts, and development of scientific knowledge about the Yellowstone area. It also sponsors the Yellowstone Association Institute, a nonprofit school, which offers a wide range of short field courses and nature study vacations year-round inside the park.

To help with other park services, the NPS has contracts with private concession companies, but the NPS authorizes prices and service rates. Xanterra Parks and Resorts (www.travelyellowstone.com) operates Yellowstone National Park Lodges and provides many park services, including lodging, dining, camping, and activity services. Delaware North Parks and Resorts (www.visityellowstonepark.com) operate the 12 Yellowstone General Stores. The seven full-service gas stations and four auto towing and repair shops in the park are operated by Yellowstone Park Service Stations (406/848-7333, www.nps.gov/yell/planyourvisit/gasstatn.htm). Yellowstone Park Medical Services (307/344-7965 year-round) operates three patient-care facilities within the park.

You can contact the NPS or concession companies at the following addresses or numbers:

DNC Parks and Resorts at Yellowstone, LLC
8358 Huffine Lane, Suite 2
Bozeman, MT 59718
406/586-7593—Yellowstone General Stores
www.visityellowstonepark.com

National Park Service
P.O. Box 168, Yellowstone National Park, WY 82190
307/344-7381
www.nps.gov

Xanterra Parks & Resorts
P.O. Box 165, Yellowstone National Park, WY 82190
307/344-7901
www.travelyellowstone.com

Yellowstone Association
P.O. Box 117, Yellowstone National Park, WY 82190
307/344-2293—books, maps, videos
Membership@yellowstoneassociation.org—membership
www.yellowstoneassociation.org

From late spring to fall there are nine places to stay in the park, with 2,200 rooms, ranging from basic to deluxe. During the winter months, the number of rooms drops to 360. Rates vary, depending upon the amenities offered. A basic cabin without bath at the Old Faithful Lodge costs $64 a night, while a suite at the Lake Yellowstone Hotel runs over $500 (rates can change).

To get the best place for your needs, reserve early (up to six months in advance during peak periods) through Xanterra Parks & Resorts, (307/344-7311 or 866/439-7375, www.travelyellowstone.com). In summer, the lodges and cabins are open early June–mid-September. In winter, the Mammoth Hot Springs Hotel and Old Faithful Snow Lodge and cabins are open late December–early March.

If you want to sleep in a tent or recreational vehicle or under the starry sky, you can choose from 2,204 campsites in 11 park campgrounds June–October. Seven are operated by the National Park Service on a first-come, first-served basis: Indian Creek, Lewis Lake, Norris, Mammoth, Pebble Creek, Slough Creek, and Tower Falls. Four campgrounds, Bridge Bay, Canyon, Grant Village, and Madison, can be reserved in advance through Xanterra Parks & Resorts. Campsites go for $17 a night depending on amenities such as flush toilets and showers. You can also reserve in advance one of 341 full-hookup sites at the Fishing Bridge RV Campground for about $35 a night. The only campground open during the winter months is located at Mammoth Hot Springs.

You can bunk down outside the park in various lodges, hotels, dude ranches, motels, and national forest campgrounds. (For more detailed information, turn to the *Lodging and Dining* or *Camping and Backpacking* chapters.)

What should we bring?

What you bring depends on where you stay and what you do in the park, but I can tell you some basic items that will make your trip more comfortable. (For advice on specific activities such as camping and hiking, turn to the *Camping and Backpacking* and *Recreational Opportunities* chapters.)

From spring through fall, our weather is hard to predict. Storms can appear suddenly, bringing rain, wind, snow, and really cold temperatures. My advice to all visitors is: Be prepared for these abrupt changes. And, whatever the season, dress in layers that you can easily add or subtract.

Most of the park is above 7,000 feet in elevation. That means the nights are always chilly, even in midsummer. It also means the ultraviolet radiation is intense, so sunscreen, sunglasses, and a hat are a must. Visitors with breathing difficulties or heart ailments may have a problem with the high elevation and extra activity. It's best to check with your physician on special precautions you can take to help prevent a heart attack or respiratory failure.

Winter arrives quickly in the park, and if you're not prepared it can be downright dangerous. Some years our first snowfall comes in October, so don't think you'll be warm enough unless you bring a warm parka, hiking boots with heavy socks, and thermal underwear. Heat escapes from your head and hands, so pack a pair of mittens and a warm cap that covers your ears.

In summer you can also save yourself some misery by bringing insect repellent. A first-aid kit is always a good idea. You'll want a pair of boots or sturdy sneakers for hiking, bicycling, or walking. Binoculars are a must if you want close-up views of our wildlife, and a camera will help you remember what you saw here. Once you're tucked away in your room, camper, or tent, it's always nice to have a good book and games to while the night away.

You can bring your pets as long as you follow some strict rules. Pets must be kept under physical control at all times, which means caged, crated, or on a leash no longer than six feet. They can go with you into the front country areas of the park, including any area within 100 feet of roads, parking areas, and campgrounds. But those are the only places they can go. They can't follow you on trails, in buildings, on boardwalks, or into the backcountry, unless they're unless they're service/assistance dogs for people with disabilities.

In the summer, you and your furry friends can pitch a tent in our campgrounds, as long as they're leashed. Pets are allowed in all of the park's cabins during summer, but they are not allowed in the other lodging facilities. Contact Xanterra Parks & Resorts (307/344-7901, www.travelyellowstone.com), the park lodging concessionaire, for further information.

The pet rules are made for good reason. Our delicate ecosystem isn't ready for the wild mountain Chihuahua or free-ranging Labrador. Just about any kind of pet could create problems for the park wildlife and their natural habitats, not to mention other visitors. The rules also help protect your pet from getting scalded to death in a thermal pool or pounded by a mother elk. We keep careful watch on these regulations, and we're not shy about handing out $25 citations to rule breakers. There are no kennel facilities for short-term boarding inside the park, but there are boarding facilities in the Greater Yellowstone Area outside the park.

Here are places to contact if you need boarding facilities outside the park:

Bozeman, Montana
All West Veterinary Hospital
406/586-4919

Bozeman Veterinary Hospital
406/587-4275

Dog on Wheels
406/763-4214

Gallatin Veterinary Hospital
406/587-4458

Kennels West
406/587-7446

Valley View Veterinary Boarding
406/586-9094

Livingston, Montana
Colmey Pet Plaza
406/222-1440

Livingston Veterinary Hospital
406/222-3011

Cody, Wyoming
Cody Veterinary Hospital
307/587-3151

Pet Set
307/587-9515

Jackson, Wyoming
Critter Sitter
307/733-1407

Jackson Hole
307/733-4279

Kindness Kennels
307/733-2633

Spring Creek Kennels
307/733-1606

FACTS ABOUT YELLOWSTONE NATIONAL PARK

- Yellowstone was the world's first national park, established on March 1, 1872.

- Administered by the U.S. Department of the Interior National Park Service, Yellowstone National Park was designated a U. S. Biosphere Reserve in 1976 and a World Heritage Site in 1978.

- Yellowstone is larger in area than Rhode Island and Delaware combined. It measures 3,472 square miles, 2,219,823 acres, 63 miles from north to south, 54 miles from east to west.

- Less than two percent of the total area of Yellowstone National Park has been developed.

- Some 95 percent of visitor use is concentrated around roads and developed areas in the park.

- Approximately five percent of the park is covered by water.

- Yellowstone is located 91 percent in Wyoming, 7.6 percent in Montana, 1.4 percent in Idaho.

- Record temperatures
  High: 98°F (Lamar, 1936)
  Low: -66°F (Madison, 1933)

- Yellowstone has
  370 miles of paved roads
  1,200 miles of developed trails
  300 designated backcountry campsites
  200-250 active geysers
  10,000 thermal features
  550 known archaeological sites
  952 historic structures

- Yellowstone Lake
  has 136 square miles of surface area
  has 110 miles of shoreline
  measures 20 miles from north to south
  measures 14 miles from east to west
  has an average depth of 139 feet
  has a maximum depth of 390 feet

- Annual visitors to Yellowstone

1872: 300	1987: 2,573,194
1892: 7,290	1990: 2,823,572
1923: 138,352	1996: 3,012,171
1948: 1,013,531	2006: 2,870,293
1957: 1,595,875	2007: 3,151,342 (record)

II.
Park
Attractions

We only have one day to visit ... what should we do?

Most rangers would tell you it takes at least three days to sample most of the wonders of Yellowstone, but here are a few tips for getting the most out of a single day.

Start by getting your bearings at one of the park's visitor centers. If you're intent on "seeing it all," take a full-day motorcoach tour around the Grand Loop Road, a figure eight–shaped road connecting the park's major scenic attractions. Along its 142 miles, you're bound to see thermal features at Mammoth Hot Springs, Norris, and the Upper Geyser Basin—the home of Old Faithful. The road crosses the Continental Divide on the way to Yellowstone Lake's West Thumb, then winds through vast Hayden Valley among herds of bison and continues on to the Grand Canyon of the Yellowstone. The motorcoaches leave from several points in the park or from Gardiner, Montana. More information, such as bus tours reservations and schedules, is available through Xanterra Parks and Resorts (307/344-7311 or 866/439-7375, www.travelyellowstone.com).

If you want a slower touring pace, I suggest you pick a few "must-sees" you'd like to explore. Then take a tour by car or motorcoach of the Upper Loop Road (starting at Mammoth and going to Norris, Canyon, Tower-Roosevelt, and back to Mammoth), or the Lower Loop Road (from Madison to Old Faithful, West Thumb, Lake Village, Canyon, Norris, and back to Madison). If you're driving, remember to leave time for walking a nature trail or having lunch at one of our lodges.

If you decide to tour the park on your own, here are some insider tips on popular attractions.

Geysers and Hot Springs
Along the 52-mile road between Mammoth Hot Springs and Old Faithful, you can access Mammoth Hot Springs, Norris Geyser Basin, Fountain Paint Pot Nature Trail, Firehole Lake Drive, Midway Geyser Basin, Biscuit Basin, and the Upper Geyser Basin, home of the famous Old Faithful Geyser. Visitor centers and interpretive exhibits are located at Mammoth Hot Springs, Norris Geyser Basin (museum), and Old Faithful.

Grand Canyon of the Yellowstone
The best features of the canyon can be seen along the 24 miles of the North and South Rim Roads in the Canyon Village area. Walk the trails along the rims and into the canyon for closer views of the Upper and Lower Falls. Tower Falls and Calcite Springs overlooks, 17 miles north of Canyon, also offer great views. Canyon Village has a visitor center and interpretive exhibit on geology.

Lake Area
With 110 miles of shoreline, Yellowstone Lake is the largest mountain lake in North America and home to a wide variety of birds and animals. Take one of the nature trails for wildlife viewing around the Mary Bay area on the north shore. Two of my favorites are the three-mile Storm Point Trail around Indian Pond and the one-mile Pelican Creek Trail. Visitor centers are located at Fishing Bridge (north shore) and Grant Village (west shore).

Wildlife Viewing

The park's major valleys—Hayden Valley, between Canyon and Fishing Bridge, and Lamar Valley, 10 miles east of Tower-Roosevelt—are great for viewing wildlife, especially in the early morning and evening hours. Lamar Valley is where packs of gray wolves can often be seen November–June.

Park History

The restored stone buildings of Fort Yellowstone date from 1891, during the army era of park administration. At the Albright Visitor Center you'll find interesting exhibits and a self-guided walking tour of the old fort, highlighting Yellowstone's colorful history.

What's the best way to get oriented?

Because Yellowstone is so big, you'll probably want to stop at one of our visitor centers to get your bearings before venturing around the park. At the centers, you can talk to a ranger, view interpretive exhibits, watch a video, browse the bookstore, and pick up current information about road conditions, hiking trails, and ranger programs in the park's five main geographic areas.

Albright Visitor Center (Mammoth Area)

Located in the former Bachelor Officers' Quarters at old Fort Yellowstone, this center (307/344-2263, year-round) houses exhibits on the early history, exploration, and establishment of Yellowstone National Park. A one-hour video, *Winter in Yellowstone*, shown in winter, will give you a taste of what winter is like in the park. In summer, an orientation film on Yellowstone is provided, as well as *The Challenge of Yellowstone*, which emphasizes history.

Old Faithful Visitor Center (Upper Geyser Basin)

The center (307/344-2750, third Fri. in Apr.–first Sun. in Nov. and mid-Dec.–mid-Mar.) is in temporary quarters near the Old Faithful Lodge until the new visitor education center is completed. Overlooking the famous geyser of the same name, you'll find plenty of exhibits to answer your questions about our geothermal attractions, including predictions of eruption times. A short movie on geysers, *Symphony of Fire and Ice*, plays throughout the day.

Canyon Visitor Education Center (Canyon Area)

Located in Canyon Village near the center of the park at Grand Canyon of the Yellowstone, this center (307/344-2550, late May/early June–Sept.) features exhibits, animations, and audio-visual productions on the geologic history of the Yellowstone volcano, its geysers and hot springs.

Grant Village Visitor Center (Yellowstone Lake West Shore)
The west shore of Yellowstone Lake is the site of a center (307/242-2650, late May/early June–Sept.) housing exhibits about the 1988 Yellowstone fires, which affected nearly a third of the park. A great film, *Ten Years After*, describes the natural regeneration process that occurs in Yellowstone every 250–400 years. You'll learn what to look for as the forests recover from the 1988 fires.

Fishing Bridge Visitor Center (Yellowstone Lake North Shore)
Housed in a National Historic Landmark building at the north end of Yellowstone Lake, this center (307/242-2450, late May/early June–Sept.) is where you'll find exhibits about the park's birds, wildlife, and lake geology. You'll also learn about unusual survival strategies used by park wildlife.

No rangers were here at the time, but we've found clues around the park that tell an ancient story of upheaval and collision. Today's Yellowstone is an artwork in progress, begun hundreds of millions of years ago with the brush strokes of fire and ice. The result is a landscape where change is constant, and the forces of nature, especially geothermal forces, are ever present.

The story starts between 3.4 billion and 600 million years ago, when huge mountain ranges formed and then eroded away, leaving Yellowstone a flat, lifeless plain. Over millions of years, floods gave life to lush jungles, then volcanic action gave birth to the Rocky Mountains. From 60 million to 40 million years ago, this fiery force helped form the Absaroka and Washburn Mountain Ranges from molten magma that covered most of the Yellowstone area.

About 600,000 years ago, tremendous volcanic blasts formed a huge crater called the Yellowstone Caldera, which today contains 47-mile-wide Yellowstone Lake. This event and the geothermal energy associated with it make Yellowstone the unique place it is today.

The Ice Age swept through Yellowstone in three glacial periods beginning 300,000 years ago. Ice caps formed, melted, and formed again at least 11 separate times. Volcanoes kept erupting through the icy crust, until whole mountains collapsed into the caldera. Fiery molten magma then seeped across the land, creating Yellowstone's overlapping plateaus. The last ice cap blanketed much of Yellowstone and helped shape the park we know today. It gouged valleys into steep-walled canyons, eroded geyser basins into open valleys on the central plateau, carved smooth cliffs, and carried rocks of all sizes across the plateaus, leaving behind long ridges and huge granite boulders as the ice melted.

Prevolcanic Stage

More than 600 million years ago, Yellowstone was a flat plain that periodically flooded to create shallow seas. For millions of years, the park looked somewhat like the Everglades in Florida. The Rocky Mountains began to rise from the plains between 75 million and 55 million years ago, bringing volcanic activity to Yellowstone.

Volcanic Stage

Volcanism begins the *big* story of how Yellowstone was formed. Volcanic activity built the Absaroka and Washburn Mountain Ranges from fiery molten lava spilling over the Yellowstone area. The Yellowstone plateau formed from the eruptions, and forests were buried by volcanic ash, creating the petrified forests we see today. The climate of Yellowstone turned hot and dry; camels, elephants, and primitive horses roamed the plains. By the end of the period, nearly two million years ago, mountain building had started again.

Caldera Stage

About 600,000 years ago, tremendous volcanic eruptions showered huge volumes of ash flow—as far away as Saskatchewan and Mississippi—creating an enormous crater and the Yellowstone plateau we know today. Called the Yellowstone Caldera, this crater was further shaped by thermal expansion, collapse, and contraction of its crust following the explosive eruptions. Today, it measures about 1,000 square miles in area, is hundreds of feet deep, and stretches 47 miles from rim to rim. From recent studies, scientists estimate that the heat below the Yellowstone Caldera is 60 times greater than the average for all other thermal areas in the world.

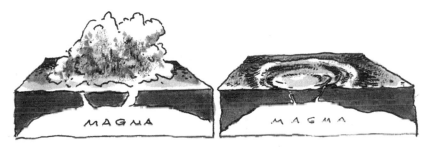

Glacial Stage

Starting about 300,000 years ago, periods of glaciation covered most of Yellowstone with ice, contrasting with the molten rock of volcanic eruptions. The last glacier, called the Pinedale Glaciation, covered most of Yellowstone with an ice cap that averaged more than 2,000 feet thick and lasted 17,000 years. It shaped Yellowstone National Park into the canyons, valleys, glacial meadows, rivers, and mountains we know today.

Why are there so many geysers in Yellowstone?

Our 200–400 active geysers are just a fraction of Yellowstone's 10,000 geothermal features—the largest, most varied collection on earth. The source lies just beneath the surface of our geyser basins, where a huge chamber of partially molten rock or *magma*, normally hundreds of miles deep, is only three miles deep. This creates an awesome heat source. Melting snow and rain seeps down into the earth through fissures in the rock, mixing with the hot magma to create boiling water. The hot water then creeps up through the hard volcanic rock, finally reaching the surface as a geyser, hot spring, fumarole, or mud pot. Here are some hints on identifying which is which.

Geysers

Geysers are hot springs that periodically erupt with great force as pressure mounts deep beneath their surface. Geyser activity changes constantly—some erupt every few seconds with minor action, like Vixen Geyser in the Norris Basin. Excelsior Geyser, in the Midway Geyser Basin, once exploded 300 feet high in the 1800s, only to remain inactive for the next 120 years. Most geysers have elaborate and varied formations around their openings. Some have mineral cones and are called *cone geysers*, like Castle Geyser in the Upper Geyser Basin. Others that erupt through a pool of water are called fountain geysers, like Great Fountain Geyser in the Lower Geyser Basin. The best known geyser in the world is Yellowstone's Old Faithful, which erupts every 30–120 minutes and spews 3,200–8,400 gallons of boiling water more than 100 feet high.

Narrow Steam Vent →

SUPERHEATED WATER UNDER PRESSURE

Hot Springs

Hot springs, or thermal pools, contain an array of colors depending upon water temperature, mineral or algae content, and absorption of light. Colors usually range from orange to blue to black. Yellowstone's largest hot spring, Grand Prismatic Spring in the Midway Geyser Basin, is 375 feet across with a deep blue color surrounded by rings of yellow and orange bacteria that create a prism effect.

HOT WATER RISES TO THE SURFACE

Fumaroles

Fumaroles, or dry geysers, are holes in the ground without enough water to be geysers. Instead, they act as steam vents that release water vapor and other gases with such power that they produce roaring, sizzling, or hissing sounds that shake the ground. The smell of rotten eggs comes from the sulfuric acid in the steam. As this is released in the air, the minerals in the steam cling to the outer edges of the vents, creating bright yellow deposits of sulfur. You can see this at sulfur vents throughout the Heart Lake Basin and at Roaring Mountain, 4.5 miles north of Norris Geyser Basin.

VENTING STEAM

Mud Pots

Another type of hot spring, the colorful mud pot or paint pot, is created when hot water mixes with clay and other minerals. In the spring and fall the paint pots are thin and soupy, and the mud bubbles and boils. In late summer they thicken and have been known to hurl hot mud 10–15 feet high. Cones will form when the mud is thick then dissolve when more water is present. You should check out the Artists' Paint Pots, located in a lodgepole pine forest at the end of a half-mile hike in the Gibbon Geyser Basin. Their multicolored palette was created when iron oxides tinted white mud with various shades of pastel beige, pink, and slate.

W e have 10,000 geothermal features and 200–400 active geysers to choose from, but hey, you have to start somewhere. To visit the most popular ones, such as Old Faithful, go in the early morning or evening to avoid big summer crowds. The ground around the geysers and hot springs is unstable and sometimes dangerously thin, so stay on the boardwalks and asphalt trails, and keep hold of your kids or parents. With those precautions, get ready to be amazed by the largest geothermal wonderland in the world.

My recommendation is to take one of our self-guiding trails through Yellowstone's geothermal features, so you can explore at your own pace. Here's a list by area in the park:

MAMMOTH AREA
Upper and Lower Mammoth Terrace Trails
You can take easy strolls (100 yards–1 mile) through the Mammoth travertine terraces from any of the four parking lots at the base of the terraces or at the Upper Terrace Loop Drive (1.5 miles from the Albright Visitor Center). Check out the beautiful pools on Minerva Terrace.

NORRIS GEYSER BASIN
Back Basin Trail (south loop)
An easy 1.5-mile round-trip passes features such as Steamboat, the world's tallest active geyser, with sporadic eruptions every few years ranging 10–300 feet. You'll also see Echinus, the largest known acid-water geyser, erupting every 35–75 minutes. Don't miss the colorful Emerald and Green Dragon Spring. Access to the trail is from the south side of the Norris Geyser Basin Museum, a great stop for more information.

Porcelain Basin Trail (north loop)
A casual 0.75-mile round trip winds through the park's oldest and hot-test thermal area. From the Norris Museum overlook, you'll experience the basin's rainbow colors, hissing steam, and pungent odors. Clay and silica minerals give the pools a milky look, and iron creates those unique orange-rimmed edges. Walk north through the breezeway at the Norris Geyser Basin Museum.

GIBBON GEYSER BASIN
Artists' Paint Pots
A one-mile round-trip hike covers a thermal area dotted with mudpots, fumaroles, and small geysers. Two mudpots at the top of the hill give you one of the park's best glimpses of these curious features. Access is 4.5 miles south of Norris at the southern end of Gibbon Meadows on the east side of the road.

LOWER GEYSER BASIN
Fountain Paint Pot
An easy 0.5-mile loop trail offers a close look at all four kinds of geothermal features in Yellowstone: mud pots, fumaroles, geysers, and hot springs. As you walk up the trail you can see how different thermal features form, based on the water table. Access is from the Lower Loop Road, eight miles south of Madison on the west side of the road.

MIDWAY GEYSER BASIN
Excelsior Geyser and Grand Prismatic Spring
An easy 0.5-mile loop on a boardwalk takes you to both Excelsior Geyser, ringed by a crater 200 feet across, and Yellowstone's largest hot spring, Grand Prismatic Spring. Access is from the Lower Loop Road, 10.5 miles south of Madison on the west side of the road.

UPPER GEYSER BASIN
Biscuit Basin Trail
An easy one-mile boardwalk trail takes you through a modest collection of small pools and geysers. Branching off the boardwalk near Avoca Spring, a moderately easy 3.5-mile loop takes you to Mystic Falls. From there, you climb 500 feet to a great scenic overlook of the Upper Geyser Basin's active geysers, including Old Faithful. Access is from the Biscuit Basin parking area, two miles north of the Old Faithful interchange on the road to Madison Junction. From the parking lot, go across the footbridge.

Observation Point Trail at Old Faithful
A one-mile loop of moderate difficulty leads to a prime place for watching Old Faithful. From Observation Point, continue on to Solitary Geyser, where you can join the Geyser Hill Loop Trail or follow the path back to the boardwalk around Old Faithful. Access is from the Old Faithful Visitor Center: walk 0.3 mile toward Old Faithful, and follow the boardwalk counterclockwise. The trail takes off from the back side of the boardwalk and crosses the Firehole River.

Lone Star Geyser Trail at Old Faithful

A five-mile easy-to-moderate round-trip goes to Lone Star Geyser's 12-foot-tall cone, the largest and most beautiful in the park. Lone Star erupts about every three hours, with blasts of up to 60 feet. Park at Kepler Cascades on the Grand Loop Road, two miles south of the Old Faithful turnoff.

WEST THUMB GEYSER BASIN/LAKE YELLOWSTONE

Two easy loops, one 0.5 mile and the other 0.25 mile, take you through the largest geyser basin on Yellowstone Lake. You'll see lots of interesting springs along the shore, including Collapsing Pool, Abyss Pool, and Fishing Cone. At Fishing Cone, anglers used to catch fish and then cook them in the hot waters of the cone. (The area is now closed to all fishing.) Park just east of the junction between the Grand Loop Road and the South Entrance Road, beside the Yellowstone Association Bookstore in the historic ranger station.

Mud Volcano Trail

An easy 0.7-mile round-trip on a boardwalk takes you past such sinister features as Black Dragon's Caldron, Sizzling Basin, and Dragon's Mouth Spring. Park off the Grand Loop Road, six miles north of Fishing Bridge.

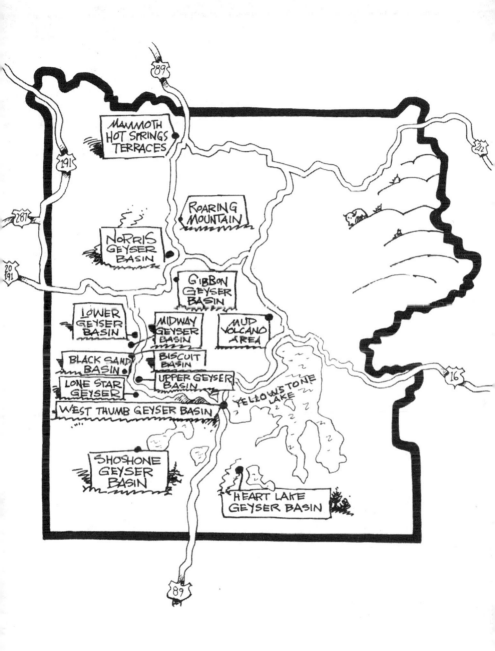

What are the Hoodoos and where can we see some?

Though the name might sound like a spook that wanders the steaming geysers at night, hoodoos are actually Yellowstone's strangely shaped rock formations mostly caused by hard, erosion-resistant rock that creates a cap on softer layers of sediment.

The name "hoodoo" was coined by a party of miners who happened upon the strange pinnacles at the head of the Lamar River. Park Superintendent P. W. Norris later referred to the formations as "monster stone-gods." Novelist Owen Wister visited the park in 1887 and wrote that the Hoodoo Basin rocks looked like "a church organ that has met with a railroad accident."

With some strenuous hiking over 28.5 miles with a 3,700-foot elevation gain from the Lamar trailhead, you can find Hoodoo Basin at the head of the Lamar River in the Absaroka Range. Another group of hoodoos can be found by Tower Falls, which is named for the pinnacles there. Similar formations, such as Chimney Rock and the Holy City, can be viewed along the North Fork of the Shoshone River east of the park toward Cody, Wyoming.

The easiest ones to find are the limestone (travertine) hoodoos, located just below and east of Terrace Mountain above Mammoth Hot Springs at Golden Gate. Here, the rocks are deposits from hot springs thousands of years old, which toppled from the east face of Terrace Mountain and settled in chaotic, leaning formations. You may see them three miles south of Mammoth Hot Springs, on the road to Norris Junction.

What's the best way to see the waterfalls?

The park's two most famous waterfalls are the Upper and Lower Falls in the Grand Canyon of the Yellowstone River. But the park has more than 230 falls and cascades to enjoy. Of the ones that are 15 feet or more, about 16 of the most spectacular can be reached from the road. If you want a bit more adventure, you'll discover the same number at the end of walks or hikes of five miles or less. And if you want a long hike, many of our waterfalls are located in remote back-country areas of the park that take a full day or an overnight hike to reach. Our falls come in all sizes and shapes, from a long, thin strand of water that drops 1,000 feet at Silver Cord Cascade in the Grand Canyon of the Yellowstone to a wall of water 250–300 feet wide that plunges 20 feet over a ledge at Cave Falls in the Bechler Falls River area in the southwest corner of the park.

Keep your eyes peeled for wildlife—many of our animals are regular visitors to the waterfalls. In the early morning or evening hours, you may catch a glimpse of a lively water ouzel in the shallow pool at Fairy Falls, an osprey flying inside the Grand Canyon near Upper and Lower Falls, a moose foraging around Moose Falls, or harlequin ducks riding the currents at LeHardy Rapids.

Here's a list of some of my favorite waterfalls and water features, grouped by area and whether you can see them from the road or by walks or hikes of five miles or less (round-trip). For more detailed information on some of these and longer day and overnight waterfall hikes, see the *Recreational Opportunities* chapter.

FIREHOLE RIVER AND BECHLER-FALLS RIVER AREA
Features that can be viewed from the roadside:
1. Cascades of the Firehole
2. Excelsior Cascade
3. Firehole Falls
4. Kepler Cascades
5. Cave Falls

Features that can be viewed with short hikes:
6. Mystic Falls, 2 miles
7. Fairy Falls, 5 miles
8. Cascade Acres, 2.5 miles
9. Terraced Falls, 3.2 miles
10. Bechler Falls, 2 miles

YELLOWSTONE AND GIBBON RIVERS, CANYON AREA
Features that can be viewed from the roadside:
11. Virginia Cascade
12. LeHardy Rapids
13. Upper Falls
14. Lower Falls

Waterfalls that can be viewed with short walks:
15. Crystal Falls, 0.25 mile
16. Lower Falls, 0.25–1 mile
17. Upper Falls, 0.25 mile

YELLOWSTONE RIVER, TOWER-ROOSEVELT AREA
Waterfalls that can be viewed from the roadside:
18. Tower Falls

Waterfalls that can be viewed with short walks:
19. Lost Creek Falls, 0.5 mile
20. Tower Falls, 0.25–1 mile

YELLOWSTONE AND GIBBONS RIVERS, MAMMOTH AREA
Features that can be viewed from the roadside:
21. Mammoth Hot Springs Terraces
22. Rustic Falls

23. Undine Falls
24. Gibbon Falls

Waterfalls that can be viewed with short walks or hikes:
25. Wraith Falls, 0.5 mile
26. Hidden Falls, 5 miles

LEWIS RIVER AREA
Waterfalls that can be viewed from the roadside:
27. Lewis Canyon Cascades
28. Lewis Falls

Waterfalls that can be viewed with short walks:
29. Moose Falls, 0.13 mile

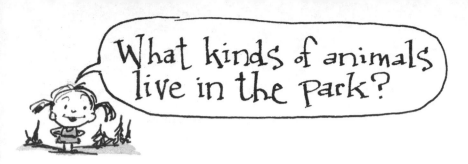

What kinds of animals live in the park?

Yellowstone is one of North America's largest wildlife havens, home to 398 different kinds of animals. It has the greatest number of wild animals in their natural habitat in the United States. With the recent restorations of peregrine falcons (1983) and gray wolves (1995), Yellowstone probably now has all of its native species—a condition found nowhere else in the lower 48 states.

If you're here between spring and fall, you'll be treated to the colors and songs of 299 species of birds. Our year-round feathered residents include the raven, trumpeter swan, bald eagle, great gray owl, and gray jay.

Eighteen species of native and non-native fish swim our rivers, streams, and lakes. We have just about every kind of trout: cutthroat, brown, rainbow, eastern brook, and lake. Six types of frogs, toads, and salamanders stay with us year-round, including the tiger salamander, western toad, and striped chorus frog. Hikers squeamish about snakes will rarely see any of our seven kinds, which include the garter snake, bullsnake, and western rattlesnake.

Most of our 64 types of mammals remain all year, which means they have to be tough to survive the deep snows and low temperatures of winter. Beasts, such as bison, and well-adapted plant eaters, such as moose and elk, cope with Yellowstone's winters by moving to places where the snow is less deep, so foraging is easier, or to thermal areas where warm ground melts much of the snow. Each year, some of our animals don't survive. Winter has always been the most common time for old and unfit animals to die in Yellowstone.

If you want to see bears, wolves, and other large animals who are not gregarious, you'll need to get up early, even before dawn, or stay out until dark for the best chances. Animals with thick fur coats are more active in the mornings and evenings, when the temperatures are cool.

Although beavers, muskrats, and otters live in the park, we don't see them a lot. Grand Teton National Park, with its many aspen- and willow-lined river habitats, is better beaver-spotting country than Yellowstone.

As you drive through the park, you'll probably see at least one of the three species in the deer family that live here: mule deer, elk or wapiti, and moose. Elk herds have the greatest numbers. They can be seen grazing in Mammoth Hot Springs, Lamar Valley, Norris Junction, and around geothermal basins. During the fall rutting season, their bugling call is heard everywhere in the park. The big mulelike ears of the mule deer make them easy to identify as they graze around Grant Village, Bridge Bay, Old Faithful, and the Lamar Valley. Bigger but more reclusive than the others, moose are the largest

antlered animals in the park; bulls weigh 800–1,200 pounds. At the end of the autumn rutting season, bulls, cows, and calves gather and stay in small areas such as Swan Lake Flat or between Fishing Bridge and Sylvan Pass. You might want to look at the moose exhibit at Willow Park, between Swan Lake Flat and Norris.

Our bison, or buffalo, are the last continuously wild and free-ranging herd in the United States. Some of their favorite grazing places include the Hayden Valley, the northern shore of Yellowstone Lake, Pelican Valley, Lamar Valley, and throughout the Lower Geyser Basin.

Of the 200–250 pronghorn antelope in the park, you may see small bands grazing at the lower elevations between Gardiner and Mammoth, toward Tower Falls and into the Lamar Valley. You may also see Rocky Mountain bighorn sheep between Gardiner and Mammoth or on a hike up Mount Washburn. In the open between Mammoth and Tower-Roosevelt and the Lamar Valley, you can see our coyotes and gray wolves.

We have two kinds of bears in the park. Black bears (sometimes brown, blond, or cinnamon-colored) weigh 135–315 pounds and spend most of their time in the more forested areas of the park. Grizzly bears (dark brown with a trace of gray at the tips), can weigh 200–700 pounds and spend most of their time in the more remote backcountry areas of the park. Hayden Valley, Lamar Valley, and Antelope Creek are good places to look for bears, particularly in May and June, at dawn or dusk. Since the 1970s, park managers have waged a successful campaign to keep our bears away from campgrounds, roadsides, and human eating places—and to keep visitors away from them. As a result, very few bears are getting into trouble by becoming habituated to human food, so they don't have to be killed.

Once you've reached the highest elevations in the park, watch for pikas, marmots, and Rocky Mountain bighorn sheep, especially on the slopes of Mount Washburn.

What are the best ways to spot wildlife?

Your chances to see Yellowstone's wildlife increase with your willingness to arrive at the right season—early summer, autumn, or winter—and to get up at dawn, when it's still cold and dark, or to linger until nearly dark.

Your car gives you a great range of mobility in Yellowstone and, since park animals are used to vehicles, can often be a good observation blind. When you arrive at an area where wildlife is visible, pull well off the road, preferably in a paved pullout. Park so that other vehicles can pass safely, and share limited pullouts. Get out of your car very quietly, without letting doors slam or engines run, and stay close to the road so the animals can predict that you won't chase them if they continue to use the area. If you're patient and willing to watch and listen silently, you may hear the bellow and grunt of a bison, the bugle of an elk, or the howl of a coyote or wolf.

The best times to see large wildlife are during the cool mornings and evenings of spring and summer and in fall and winter. Like people, animals seek out the most comfortable times of day to explore. Remember, the big animals all wear thick fur coats.

In the spring and summer, Yellowstone is literally for the birds. Birders are well advised to leave their cars behind, get away from the roads, and become bird listeners, as a thousand songs fill the air. Among our rare species, bald eagles are often spotted flying above Yellowstone Lake or along the Madison, Snake, or Yellowstone Rivers. Visitors often see graceful, snowy-white trumpeter swans year-round along the Madison River or the Yellowstone River as it winds through Hayden Valley.

Dark fabrics blend more naturally with the surroundings. If you're walking, move slowly; if you see an animal, avoid sudden movements. Don't forget

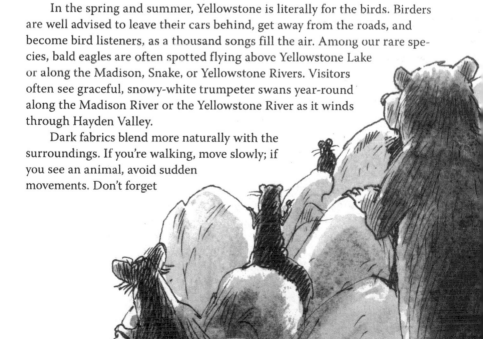

binoculars: They're an essential tool in a park the size of Yellowstone, especially if you're viewing animals from your car or the road. A spotting scope can reach even farther. Just remember that park regulations prohibit visitors from approaching animals at a distance closer than 25 yards (100 yards for bears).

Since "cold-blooded" reptiles depend upon warm weather to survive, we don't have many in Yellowstone. Except for the poisonous prairie rattlesnake, found in the lower Yellowstone and Gardiner River canyons, our reptiles (including the Rocky Mountain rubber boa, the bull snake, and the western terrestrial garter snake) are harmless.

If you want to glimpse some of Yellowstone's 18 kinds of fish, approach the task with the care and timing of a master angler. Waiting beside a lake or stream spring–fall, you can watch them feeding, making ripples in the still waters of early morning or late afternoon.

Chipmunks, ground squirrels, and red squirrels are easy to find at most elevations late spring–fall. Around your campground or picnic area you may see them gathering seeds or crumbs—perhaps food left on the table. You can see coyotes year-round hunting mice from the late afternoon on into the evening in Lamar Valley. After coyote pups are born in April, the whole family goes hunting on late summer evenings, and their howls and yips resound through our backcountry areas. In the early evening, you may see mule deer foraging on the park's open sage-covered slopes, especially around the north entrance near Gardiner, Montana.

Bison herds roam year-round in the Madison-Firehole River and Old Faithful Thermal Basins, along the northern shore of Lake Yellowstone, in Pelican Valley, and in Lamar and Hayden Valleys. Driving through Hayden Valley, you'll probably see hundreds of bison. If you're here in the mating season (late July–early August), you might see bulls charge each other in heated battles. That's an especially good time to keep your distance.

Elk move in large herds, grazing in the Madison, Lamar, and Hayden Valleys. In the fall, you can hear elk bugling all over the park, heralding the start of the mating season. Elk have always been abundant in the park. Today, we may have 30,000 elk during the summer months and 20,000 in the winter. They form eight herds, which graze throughout the park in the summer and migrate to lower areas in the winter.

While bison and elk are gregarious, moose are more solitary. You may see one near Yellowstone Lake, in the shallows of the Yellowstone River in Hayden Valley, or in willow flats near Indian Creek, Slough Creek, or the Snake River.

You'll have to be pretty fast to keep up with our antelope, or pronghorn. They can sprint 45–50 miles per hour. Small herds of pronghorn graze year-round along the gravel road north of the Roosevelt Arch near Gardiner, Montana and roam Lamar Valley and Swan Lake Flat in the summer.

Most of our grizzly and black bears are surprisingly shy, but they can be fierce when people get too close. Although you'll seldom see bears along the roads, you may encounter them almost anywhere in the park. In the winter, both black and grizzly bears sleep in partial hibernation November–April. For safety, we prohibit visitors from approaching these animals.

In fact, don't try to get close to any animals in the park. Remember, all of our animals are wild, especially when it comes to interactions with people. Play it safe, and use binoculars for an up-close look at wildlife in Yellowstone.

BISON: FACTS AND ISSUES

- The terms *buffalo* and *bison* are both acceptable names for the bison in Yellowstone.
- Bison have inhabited the Greater Yellowstone Area since prehistoric times.
- Between 1870 and 1880 the Yellowstone bison herd became increasingly isolated, as more than 60 million buffalo were hunted and killed in other parts of the country.
- In 1902, 21 bison were transported to Yellowstone National Park to be interbred with the remnant native bison herd.
- Today, the Yellowstone herd consists of approximately 3,500 animals and remains a national symbol of wildlife preservation efforts and a focus of scientific interest.
- Outside the park, there are over 150,000 bison in public and private herds in the United States and Canada.
- Bison can weigh 2,000 pounds and still sprint at 30 miles per hour.
- In Yellowstone, bison prefer to feed on sedges and grasses; they seldom eat shrubs and forbs. Thermal areas are their favorite winter feeding grounds.
- Bison are quite gregarious, especially when there's plenty to eat. Yet they can be unpredictable and dangerous. Old males (bulls) are often the least tolerant of human activity. *Never approach bison.*
- Although stolid in personality, bison are not stupid. Experts generally agree that bison can be made to do only what they want to do.
- Bison migrate onto public and private lands beyond the park's boundaries, usually in search of food during winter months. Because humans now occupy much of what used to be bison habitat, conflicts occur.
- There is a huge debate over the management of Yellowstone bison because they can cause considerable damage to fences, crops, landscaping, and other private property, and about 12-20 percent of them are infected with brucellosis, a disease that can also infect cattle and elk.
- An interagency bison management plan has been developed jointly by Yellowstone National Park, Gallatin National Forest, the Montana Department of Livestock, and the Montana Department of Fish, Wildlife, and Parks, with the help of the U.S. Department of Agriculture's Animal and Plant Health Inspection Service. For more information and updates on the plan, call the National Park Service Public Affairs Office (307/344-2013).

To learn more about bison, read one of the books listed in the *Further Reading* section of the *Quick Reference* chapter.

D on't do it. Every time someone feeds an animal in the park, a little bit of the "wild" is stolen from our wildlife. Human food may not only damage the animals' health but also endanger their survival by luring them away from their natural habits—and into the roads!

Feeding a chipmunk or ground squirrel might seem like fun, but these creatures can carry plague. Feeding elk or deer makes them less wary of humans, and they may kick or gore someone. Watch out for the ravens, who are adept at getting food from backpacks and snowmobiles, and coyotes, who may attack those who try to feed them.

Our bears provide the best example of how much damage is done when visitors feed animals. When the park's grizzlies and black bears became protected species in 1883, visitors started feeding them, and food was left for them to eat in the park garbage dumps. Gradually, many bears became dependent on humans and their food. Instead of hunting and scavenging native foods—such as elk, bison, trout, and grass—the bears ate biscuits, steak scraps, cookies, ice cream, and sometimes plastic and foil. They started begging from roadsides, where visitors gathered around to feed them. The result: During the period 1931–1969, an average of 46 people were injured annually, and an average of 22 black bears and three grizzly bears had to be killed each year. The National Park Service adopted a program in the late 1960s to restore the natural habits of the bears. We closed the park garbage dumps, installed "bear-proof" garbage cans, taught campers how to store food safely, and began giving citations to visitors who broke the rules. Today, the bears are again healthy, wild, and self-sustaining, with cubbing rates up and the overall population stable or slightly on the rise. What's more, few people are hurt by bears or have property damaged by them.

Federal law now prohibits people from feeding or approaching the park's wildlife and for good reason. Our animals may look harmless, but any one of them is capable of causing infection, injury, and in extreme cases even death to people who get too close. If an animal reacts to your presence, you're probably too close.

> **Is there anything we need to know about bears in Yellowstone?**

Yellowstone National Park is one of the few places in the lower 48 states that is home to both black bears and grizzly bears. The two types share many traits:

- Both have a natural curiosity, good memory, acute sense of smell, good eyesight and color vision, and excellent hearing. They stand on their hind legs to heighten their senses of smell, sight, and hearing.
- Bears can run uphill or downhill at more than 35 miles per hour.
- Bears are omnivores, but plants make up much of their diet. Fish and meat are important sources of protein and fat.
- In the spring, bears feed on winter-killed elk, elk calves, bison, rodents, insects, grasses, clovers, dandelions, and other plants.
- In the summer, bears add thistle, fireweed, bistort, roots, mushrooms, spawning cutthroat trout, strawberries, and other berries to their diet.
- In the fall, bears eat roots and dense groups of moths in high-elevation areas, as well as whitebark pine nuts, plants, berries, ants, and elk injured or killed in rutting season.
- Males and females come together briefly for breeding in summer and remain separate the rest of the year.
- Breeding season is mid-May–mid-July, with most mating occurring during June. Delayed implantation keeps fertilized eggs from starting to develop until around the start of hibernation.
- Cubs are born in January or February, usually two to a litter, but the litter can range from one to four. Play is important to cubs for social and physical development and just plain fun. Subadult females tend to stay within their mother's home range, while males usually leave the range completely.
- From spring to fall, bears sleep outside, not in dens or caves.
- In winter (Oct./Nov.–Mar./Apr.), bears hibernate in dens or caves because of a decreased food supply, not because they can't stay warm.

- Each season, males emerge from their dens first, with females and cubs emerging later.
- Dens are lined with leaves, spruce and fir boughs, and pine needles.
- During hibernation, bears metabolize their fat and don't eat, urinate, or defecate for up to six months. They lose up to 40 percent of their body weight, their heart rates drop from 40 or 50 beats per minute during summer sleep to 8 or 10 beats per minute, and their body temperatures drop only a few degrees. Unlike rodents, bears can be easily aroused from their winter sleep.

What's the difference between Grizzly Bears and Black Bears?

There are several ways to tell a grizzly from a black bear. Grizzly bear color varies from blond to black with light-tipped (grizzled) fur on the head and upper body. The black bear can be black, brown, blond, or cinnamon color, but about half are black with a light brown snout.

A grizzly's average weight is 350 pounds for males and 275 pounds for females, with some males weighing up to 700 pounds. The average weight for a black bear is 135–315 pounds, with males usually larger than females. A grizzly is about 3.5 feet high at the shoulder on all fours and 6–7 feet tall standing upright. A black bear is 2.5–3 feet at the shoulder on all fours and five feet standing upright. Grizzly bears have a distinctive shoulder hump, which provides powerful muscle mass for digging. The rump of a black bear is higher than its front shoulders.

A grizzly has a dished-in profile between its eyes and snout, while the black bear's face is straight with a long muzzle. The ears of a grizzly are round and fairly small, while the black bear's are long and prominent. The grizzly's front claws are around four inches long, slightly curved, and good for digging. The black bear's claws are less than two inches long, curved, and good for climbing; its claw marks are not always seen in tracks.

DISHED FACE PROFILE

HUMP

LONG LIGHTER CLAWS

· Grizzly Bear·

Although grizzlies often avoid people by living in rugged and remote areas, they are generally more aggressive than black bears, especially when surprised. Grizzly bears are stronger and can kill an adult bull moose or elk with one swipe of a front paw. Grizzlies are most active between dusk and dawn, while black bears are mainly active from dawn to dusk, but both are potentially active anytime. The grizzly bear is a powerful digger and feeds on roots, bulbs, and rodents, while the black bear is an excellent tree climber and eats nuts and fruits in trees. The grizzly makes its den on steep mountain slopes, while the black bear often makes its den under tree roots at low to middle elevations. Grizzly cubs weigh about one pound at birth and stay with their mother 2.5–3.5 years, while black bear cubs weigh about 0.5 pound at

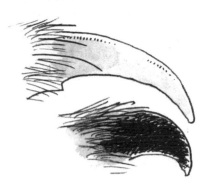

Grizzly claws are up to 4 inches long and light in color. Black bear claws are shorter, darker and curved—ideal for tree climbing.

STRAIGHT FACE PROFILE

NO HUMP

RUMP HIGHER THAN SHOULDERS

LIGHTER SNOUT

SHORTER DARKER CLAWS

·Black Bear·

birth and stay with their mother only 1.5 years.

Nearly 100,000 grizzlies once ranged in the plains, forests, mountains, shorelines, and wetlands from the Missouri River to the Pacific Ocean and from Canada to Central Mexico. Fewer than 1,000 grizzlies exist today in the lower 48 states, occupying less than one percent of their former range. They are listed as a threatened species. Grizzly bears currently inhabit five or six remote areas in Montana, Wyoming, Idaho, and Washington.

Black bears once ranged from the Atlantic to the Pacific Oceans and from the tree line in the Arctic to northern Mexico. Black bears inhabit 75 percent of their former range in 40 of the 48 contiguous states, and they are not listed as threatened. Black bears show more of a tendency to live near people and are returning to many forested areas near major cities.

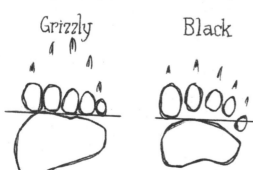

Grizzly

Black

Grizzly tracks differ from black bear tracks. The toe prints are in a straighter line and the claws extend far from the toes.

Is it true that bears are the most dangerous animals in the park?

Does it surprise you to learn that three times as many visitors are gored by bison than are attacked by grizzly and black bears combined? Our bison seem slow, but they're actually fast. They can run up to 40 miles per hour, armed with sharp hoofs and horns that can strike swiftly and without warning. Most dangerous is a lone bull during mating season or a cow protecting her calves.

Most injuries in the park result from people trying to get too close to animals, like when they try to feed the squirrels by hand and end up getting scratched or bitten. Fleas carried by ground squirrels have been known to spread disease—even bubonic plague. So don't be fooled into thinking the little cute ones are harmless.

And though our wolves and coyotes show some resemblance to your dog friends back home, they are wild and should be avoided.

With a natural fear of humans, mountain lions pose little threat to people in the park. These federally protected animals feed mostly on deer, a natural activity that helps keep our ecology in a delicate balance.

Because of their habits and imposing sizes, Yellowstone's grizzly and black bears are potentially dangerous. But most of the danger can be avoided.

Three Situations Visitors Need To Avoid:

- Surprising bears at close range or when they are eating
- Approaching a female with cubs or "stalking" a grizzly to get a closer photograph
- Attempting to take back a food package that a bear has claimed

Making bears aware of your presence and then giving them room is your best protection. Let's just say it's best if people and bears maintain a "long-distance" relationship.

WOLVES IN YELLOWSTONE

- Wolves were part of the post-Ice Age fauna of Yellowstone, as documented by paleontological evidence.

- Wolves roamed Yellowstone from at least 1,000 years ago until the 1930s, when they were hunted and mostly eradicated by government hunters.

- After an absence of more than 50 years, wolves were reintroduced into Yellowstone National Park in the winter of 1995 with the release of 14 gray wolves. Another 17 were released in 1996.

- At the end of 2006, at least 136 wolves (76 adults, 60 pups) in 13 packs were living in Yellowstone. In 2007, we had 171 wolves in 11 packs.

- The wolf recovery goal of restoring 10 packs of wolves reproducing in Yellowstone for three successive years was met in 2003.

- The restoration of wolves is in keeping with national park goals to perpetuate all native species and their natural habitats.

- Winter studies in 2006 documented 281 wolf kills, including 219 elk (80%), 30 bison (11%), 6 coyotes, 5 wolves, 3 deer, 2 bighorn sheep, 2 moose, 1 beaver, 1 golden eagle, and 12 unknown prey (www.nps.gov/yell/naturescience/wolves.htm).

- Wolves are born blind and open their eyes after about nine days. Their eyes are blue at first but turn yellow as they mature.

- Wolves are very territorial. They hunt in packs, with the alpha male or female as the leader. Wolves leave their original pack after 1-3 years to start another pack.

- Wolf howling is a form of communication. It is often used by lone wolves trying to locate their packs or to warn other wolves.

- Wolves can run as fast as 35 miles per hour.

- Wolves pose no threat to human safety. No wild, healthy wolf has been documented to have killed a human in North America. However, they are large, powerful predators that should be respected.

- Wolves may attack dogs because they see dogs as trespassers in their territory.

See *Yellowstone Today* for interpretive programs on wolves, or call the Yellowstone Association Institute at 307/344-2294 for a catalog with courses on wolves (www.yellowstoneassociation.org).

Any great birding spots?

No matter where you go in the Greater Yellowstone Area, you're likely to see birds. Although you'll find the greatest diversity of birds early June–early July and mid-August–mid-September, the rest of the year can be special for birding too. Chances to see rare, unusual, or elusive birds arise during the spring (early May–mid-June) and fall (mid-Aug.–early Nov.) migrations. The annual Audubon Christmas bird count in the Mammoth area happens one day during the last two weeks of December or first week of January.

For the best birding in Yellowstone, check out the five areas described below. You can reach them easily from park roads or walking trails, and all of the birds can be seen in the summer months. For more information on the walking trails, refer to the *Recreational Opportunities* chapter.

Mammoth Area

Look for birds such as the red-tailed hawk, golden eagle, killdeer, hairy woodpecker, mountain chickadee, red-breasted nuthatch, and common raven as you drive along the Mammoth-Gardiner Road, Old Gardiner Road, Upper Terrace Drive, and Bunsen Peak Road. Good birding walks include the Main Terrace Trails, Beaver Pond Loop Trail, the area around the Mammoth Museum and Headquarters at Fort Yellowstone, Mammoth Campground, and the Bunsen Peak Trail.

Fishing Bridge, Lake Yellowstone Area

As you walk along the shore of Lake Yellowstone around the Fishing Bridge Museum, keep an eye out for a large number of birds, including the common loon, American white pelican, Canada goose, mallard, osprey, bald eagle, California gull, and common raven. Other great birding walks are at Fishing Bridge, Elephant Back Loop Trail, Lake Hotel waterfront, Storm Point Loop Trail, and Pelican Creek Nature Trail in the Mary Bay area. If you're driving through the area, try the Pelican Creek pullout, Indian Pond overlook, Fishing Bridge pullout, and Lake Hotel waterfront.

Tower-Roosevelt Area

You might see the ring-necked duck, red-tailed hawk, red-naped sapsucker, American dipper or water ouzel, and mountain bluebird as you drive from Tower to Tower Falls, Junction Butte Ponds, or Blacktail Plateau Drive or from Blacktail Plateau Drive to Petrified Tree Drive. Great birding walks include Lost Lake Trail, Petrified Tree Trail, Tower Falls Trail, Roosevelt Lodge and vicinity, Yellowstone Picnic Area Trail, and the Garnet Hills-Hellroaring Trails.

Canyon Area

One of our most dramatic areas for bird-watching is the Grand Canyon of the Yellowstone. It's also the best place to see ospreys nesting on rock pinnacles. Other birds you might spot include the Swainson's hawk, American kestrel, great gray owl, northern flicker, cliff swallow, gray jay, chipping sparrow, and dark-eyed junco. Good birding drives are along North Rim Drive, Inspiration Point Drive, South Rim Drive, Canyon-Hayden Valley Drive, and Cascade Meadow. On foot, try the North Rim Trail, South Rim Trail, and Uncle Tom's Trail.

Mount Washburn Area

To see birds in this area, you have to do some hiking. The walk to the top of Mount Washburn (10,243 ft.) is strenuous, but you don't have to reach the summit to enjoy the birding. The two main trails are easily accessed from parking areas. One starts at the Chittenden Road parking area and the other at Dunraven Pass. On these trails you may see the Cooper's hawk, northern goshawk, blue grouse, olive-sided flycatcher, tree swallow, Steller's jay, Clark's nutcracker, water pipit, and hermit thrush. Good birding is found along the Chittenden Road Trail. Although the hike is only three miles each way, it's steep, so the round-trip takes 3–6 hours. Be sure to pack warm clothing, food, sunscreen, and drinking water, and avoid the hike if heavy clouds are gathering because lightning on the mountain can be dangerous.

Enough about animals... what kind of flora will we see?

Follow me.

Just as the animal populations change in Yellowstone, so do the plants. To sample Yellowstone's vast array of plant life, let's take a tour of seven different plant habitats, or communities, in the park. We'll start at the water's edge, then move from the lowest elevations to the highest areas, where you wouldn't think anything could survive.

Wherever there's still or flowing water in the park—near streams, rivers, lakes and marshes—you'll find aquatic plants, including water hemlock (which is poisonous), yellow pond lily, buttercup, watercress, and various grasses. Good viewing areas are Lake Yellowstone, the Lamar River, and Willow Park.

Near the north entrance around Mammoth and Gardiner, Montana, you'll notice a large area of sagebrush flats at the lowest park elevations. These open grasslands and desert plants get only about 12 inches of rain per year. In the lowest elevations, you'll find "cold desert" plants such as rabbitbrush, greasewood, junegrass, and needle and thread. In the higher areas, look for grassland plants, such as sagebrush and Rocky Mountain juniper; you'll also find some cottonwood trees along the Gardiner River. The sagebrush comes in several species, which are eaten by bighorn sheep, deer, and sage grouse for their rich stores of protein and fat.

The forests rule in Yellowstone, covering about 80 percent of the park. The Douglas-fir forest grows at an elevation of 6,000–7,600 feet on the road between Mammoth Hot Springs and Tower-Roosevelt. These woodland areas consist of mostly mature, scattered, and fire-scarred Douglas-fir and some white-barked quaking aspen, with an undergrowth of snowberry, pinegrass, and wildflowers, among which lupine is often prominent.

Geothermal areas such as Lower Geyser Basin play host to a variety of plants, including yellow monkeyflowers. Around the boardwalks at Old Faithful, look for common fringed gentian and yellow monkeyflower.

Lodgepole pine forests at elevations of 7,000–8,500 feet cover about

50 percent of the park. Unlike the Douglas-fir forests, these densely packed woods look like a sea of green around Yellowstone Lake and on the south side of Mount Washburn. Some of the trees depend on heat from forest fires to pop open their cones and release seeds, which germinate, sprout, and start new lodgepole pine forests.

In the subalpine meadows at 8,400–10,000 feet, you're likely to find summer's grassy blankets of richly colored wildflowers, including the glacier lily, spring beauty, buttercup, and fireweed in burned areas. Look for spruce-fir forests around the meadows, especially in the area from Canyon Village to the Upper Falls, the upper slopes of Mount Washburn, and along the shores of Yellowstone Lake. These high-elevation forests are filled with Engelmann spruce, subalpine fir, and whitebark pine trees.

Above the tree line, at 10,000 feet, you'll find our alpine tundra. Look carefully for tiny mats of wildflowers. The plants at this elevation grow low to the ground, limited by snowbanks, freezing temperatures, and year-round strong winds.

Other trees are found in fewer numbers throughout the park. These include many species of willows along stream bottoms (most are shrubs rather than trees), cottonwoods around Mammoth Hot Springs and in the northern part of the park, a few aspen around rivers and streams, also in the northern part of the park, and limber pines around Mammoth.

Where are the best places to see wildflowers?

Our long, severe winters limit the park's growing season, but in the peak months of June, July, and August, you'll see a spectacular display of wildflowers at every elevation and type of habitat.

The first and last flowers to bloom are found in the thermal areas and below the 7,500-foot elevation around Mammoth and Gardiner. Looking carefully around the sagebrush areas in the northern part of the park, you'll find the sagebrush buttercup, prickly pear, death camas, wild geranium, Indian paintbrush, phlox, a dozen species of lupine, larkspur, and Montana's state flower, bitterroot.

As you travel higher in elevation, explore the meadows, canyons (Sheepeater), and valleys (Hayden and Pelican Creek) in the park to see the delicate flowers that bloom during June's snowmelt and recede with the first snow flurries of late August. Look for beds of spring beauty, phlox, Jacob's ladder, buttercup, and paintbrush. In the upland meadows, you may find asters, glacier lilies, and penstemons, among others. Lupine blooms beneath lodgepole pines, and yellow columbines and mountain bluebells line the streams. Along the road over Dunraven Pass, look for the mountain bluebell, the showy green gentian, paintbrushes, and monkeyflowers, and in the Lamar Valley the lupine and sticky geranium. Around Old Faithful, keep an eye out for golden aster near the buildings and fringed gentian near the boardwalks.

At the highest elevations, above 10,000 feet, look for sky pilot, alpine forget-me-not, daisies, paintbrush, and American bistort, among others.

Here are a few of my favorite wildflower walks and areas in the park:

- The trail to Hidden Falls
- The 175-yard trail on the south side of the Lewis River to Lewis Falls
- In and around Sheepeater Canyon
- The trail to Fairy Falls
- The meadows around Union Falls
- The trail up to the summit of Mount Washburn

And here are some hints on what to look for as you travel around the park:

- The pondlily or wokas, the only large yellow flower floating on Yellowstone waters
- The reddish purple monkeyflower, while you travel over Dunraven Pass
- The purple sky pilot and yellow groundsel along the Mount Washburn Trail
- The blue lupine and pink sticky geranium in open areas
- The yellow daisylike helianthella flowers that grow in meadows near aspen trees
- The white clusters of cow parsnip in the open meadows that provide food for our bear, elk, and deer
- The tall, pink elephant's head in wet areas throughout the park

Yellow Columbine

Where are the best places to see fall color?

To tell you the truth, Yellowstone wouldn't be my first choice. We do have cottonwoods, especially in the Lamar Valley, and aspens along the Blacktail Plateau and in higher elevations, which turn golden in the fall, but they're scattered in small pockets. In the Greater Yellowstone Area, the best place to see fall color is Jackson Hole along the Snake River Valley in Grand Teton National Park. From late August through October, cottonwoods, willows, and aspens ignite that valley into an expanse of gold. But watch out—by late October or early November you could get hit by the first winter snows.

Leave Yellowstone via the south entrance road, and follow the Snake River as it winds its way through Teton National Forest, along the shores of Jackson Lake, and down the broad valley known as Jackson Hole. This valley is also home to a string of lakes in glacier-carved basins, and the wildlife and wildflowers are abundant.

As you drive toward the town of Jackson on Hwy. 89, stop to look around at the awesome landscape. The Snake River overlook gives a great overall view of the valley, the river, and the mountains. Other places to stop include Teton Point turnout, Schwabacher Landing Road, and Blacktail Ponds overlook. One of the great roads for viewing wildlife and fall color is the back road that partially follows the Snake River from Moose to Wilson. Be prepared to drive slowly, rambling for part of the way along a dirt road.

Where can we see a petrified forest?

You can start your tour of Yellowstone's famous "forests of stone" at the petrified tree on the Grand Loop Road one mile west of Tower Junction. Then you can move five miles east of that junction to Specimen Ridge or to the Gallatin Petrified Forest, north of the park. It's all part of the most extensive fossil forest in the world. Some of the petrified trees in this 40-square-mile forest are standing in the same positions in which they grew millions of years ago, and some are so well preserved that botanists can still identify them.

The story of Specimen Ridge begins about 50 million years ago, when two chains of volcanoes erupted over a period of three million years, causing widespread mudflows that buried mountains and forests. Over tens of millions of years, the volcanic ash was eroded by rain, snow, and wind. Recent studies of the Specimen Ridge area have revealed as many as 27 separate levels of fossilized trees. You can see the forest along a three-mile walk with a steep 1,100-foot climb. The easiest access is from a service road that leaves the northeast entrance road a few hundred yards west of the Lamar River Bridge and about five miles from Tower Junction.

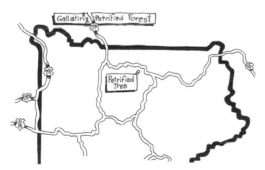

Just 10–15 miles outside the park's northwest corner, there's a short day hike along a well-defined trail that takes you into the Gallatin Petrified Forest above Tom Miner Campground. Here, if you get a permit, you're allowed to collect up to 20 cubic inches of petrified wood. Interpretive signs along the trail give you clues to the events that created the forest, as you pass petrified logs and wood fragments exposed in the bluffs northwest of the campground. For trail and permit information, contact the Gallatin National Forest Ranger Station (406/848-7375 or 406/848-7376) in Gardiner, Montana.

What was life like for Yellowstone's native people?

Imagine Yellowstone long before it was a national park: no cars or roads, no buildings or parking lots, but geysers, gushing waterfalls, golden meadows, abundant bighorn sheep, deer, elk, and bison herds.

Since the last Ice Age, about 8,500 years ago, the only people in the Yellowstone area were nomadic people. Then about 600 years ago, the region became home and hunting ground for Native American tribes of the Great Plains, such as the Crow, Blackfoot, Shoshone, Bannock, Nez Perce, Paiute, and Flathead. Of these, only one lived here year-round—the small Shoshone tribe called the Tukarika, or Sheepeaters, whose primary food was the bighorn sheep.

The Tukarika spent summers in the high alpine meadows and mountain passes, where they hunted bighorn and other animals, fished the streams and high mountain lakes, and gathered roots and berries. They hunted with bows and obsidian arrows, cooked over fires, tanned hides for clothing, and built bark or brush wickiups as summer homes. In winter, they sought shelter in protected canyons or caves. They had no horses but used dogs to help carry their few possessions from camp to camp and used geysers to help soften sheep horns so that they could be made into bows.

The small family camps of Tukarika adapted well to the harsh environment. The people asked nothing more than clothing, shelter, and a full belly. They lived near good hunting areas and did their best to avoid confrontations with the more warlike tribes who occasionally entered their remote mountain locations.

By the mid-1800s, the Tukarika had been reduced to dozens by warring tribes, fur traders and mountain men, and a smallpox epidemic. In 1871, when the Hayden Expedition entered the Yellowstone area, the last of the tribe left Yellowstone to join other Shoshone people on the Wind River Reservation in Wyoming.

Reminders of the area's Native American tribes still remain. The name Yellowstone comes from the Sioux word *Mi tse a-da-zi*, the tribe's name for the Yellowstone River; the first Europeans in the area translated this as "yellow rock river." You can still see the Bannock Trail, used by various Native American tribes in search of bison hunting grounds, as you travel through parts of Yellowstone. It enters the park from Targhee Pass in Idaho near West Yellowstone and goes up the Gallatin Range into Indian Creek. It then follows the present route of the road between Mammoth and Cooke City, Montana, at the northeast entrance to the park. Various Native American hearth sites, stone circles, and even wickiups have been discovered in remote areas of the park. Other references to the area's first inhabitants can be seen in park names such as Sheepeater Cliffs, Shoshone Lake, Wahhi Falls, and Sheepeater Canyon.

To learn more about Yellowstone's native peoples, visit the Colter Bay Indian Arts Museum in Grand Teton National Park. From June to September, you can see an extensive private collection of artifacts and craft demonstrations by Native Americans there. For more information, contact the Colter Bay Visitor Center (307/739-3594).

When did the first Euro-American pioneers come to Yellowstone?

Would-be Yellowstone explorers Lewis and Clark got only as close as the Livingston-Bozeman Area in 1805. John Colter, a member of the Lewis and Clark Expedition, returned to the area in 1807 to advise neighboring American Indian tribes of the location of the Missouri Fur Trading Company at the mouth of the Big Horn River. Colter became the first known Euro-American to enter the area known today as Yellowstone National Park.

Others soon followed, beginning an era of fur trapping, trading, and tales of steam-spitting geysers and wildlife beyond imagination. Legendary mountain men such as Jim Bridger made quite an impression, leaving their names on some of our landmarks: Bridger Mountains, Bridger Wilderness, Bridger-Teton National Forest, and Bridger Lake.

As the era of the mountain men came to a close in the 1840s, many of these trappers became trail guides for pioneer wagon trains and a growing number of government explorations of the West. The westward movement along the Oregon Trail diverted attention from the Greater Yellowstone Area between 1840 and the late 1860s, but eventually some major expeditions were launched to explore and map the area scientifically.

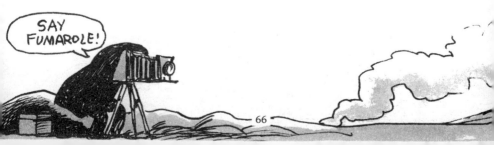

SAY FUMAROLE!

Henry Washburn, surveyor of the Montana Territory, organized an excursion in 1870 that put Mount Washburn, several other mountains, and many other well-known features on the map of Yellowstone.

News of the Washburn expedition reached Dr. Ferdinand Hayden, director of the U.S. Geological and Geographical Survey, who convinced Congress to pay for the first of four expeditions. Hayden assembled a distinguished group of scientists, artist Thomas Moran, and photographer William Jackson. The result was an exhaustive survey, several maps, and the first photographs and sketches of the area, proving that those improbable tales of natural wonders were true. Hayden rallied in Washington for protection of the Yellowstone region, and, in 1872, President Ulysses S. Grant signed a law establishing a "public park and pleasuring ground for the benefit and enjoyment of the people." Yellowstone National Park was born.

To learn more about the history of the national park, stop by the Albright Visitor Center (307/344-2263) at Mammoth and tour the historical exhibits.

What role did the Army play in the history of Yellowstone?

In response to years of complaints, from the time the park was established in 1872, the U.S. Army entered Yellowstone in 1886 to manage the area, enforce regulations, and protect park resources from vandals and poachers. Within a few years the army had built Fort Yellowstone at Mammoth Hot Springs and the Secretary of the Interior began to establish a slew of regulations against poaching, raising the ire of those who were making a good living off the park's wildlife.

The army built cabins throughout the park for year-round patrolling and law enforcement. It undertook a survey of the park's features, counting wildlife and monitoring geyser activity, among other tasks. But rampant poaching of Yellowstone's bison and elk herds was hard to prevent, especially during the winter. By 1894, illegal poaching had reduced the country's last wild bison herd to fewer than 100 animals. Things got so bad that, in 1902, the army rounded up most of the remaining 25 bison and moved them to fenced areas at Mammoth and Lamar where they could be monitored, bred, and fed in the winter. The old bison ranch in the Lamar Valley is now a ranger station and educational center.

In addition to protecting wildlife, the soldiers fought fires, curbed vandalism by tourists, and achieved such major accomplishments as completion of the Grand Loop Road in 1905. Three years after seeing the first autos roll through the gates on August 1, 1915, the army handed the reigns of park management over to the newly formed National Park Service.

The army's 32 years of service in the park helped preserve and protect Yellowstone's resources and paved the way for park management in the years to come.

Upper Basin Soldier Station c. 1895

Are there any plants or areas we should avoid?

In Yellowstone, bears and bison aren't the only park residents you should avoid. A few of our plants have a nasty bite, but, if you use a little extra caution hiking the trails and exploring the geyser basins, you won't be bringing home a rash full of memories.

Poisonous water hemlock grows in still and flowing water throughout the park, and yellow-flowered spurge grows as tall as three feet around the warm vapors of our geothermal areas in the winter. This spurge contains a milky substance that can cause a rash around the mouth and eyes, if rubbed on the face, and in extreme cases can cause blindness. Other plants to steer clear of include stinging nettles, poison ivy (rare), cacti, and raspberries, gooseberries, roses, and thistles, which can prick you.

At least two poisonous gases occur naturally in the park's thermal areas and the caves in the Mammoth area. One is hydrogen sulfide, the other carbon dioxide. Although quantities in most areas are low enough to be harmless, in an area called Death Gulch in northeast Yellowstone, higher concentrations of hydrogen sulfide have been known to kill animals, including grizzlies. Higher concentrations of carbon dioxide have killed birds, insects, and small animals in some of the small thermal caves in the Mammoth area, including Devil's Kitchen, McCartney's Cave, Poison Cave and Spring, and the Stygian Caves. To be sure, hikers should stay clear of crevices, basins, or caves where heavier-than-air gases can accumulate.

What can I take home as a memento of my visit?

With the awe-inspiring backdrop of Yellowstone, anyone with a camera can take home some of the magic without stealing a piece of the park's beauty. There are no mementos quite like the photographs that capture and give life to your own special memories, such as a summer walk through meadows of wildflowers to the top of Mount Washburn, a hike to Osprey Falls, or seeing a sunrise over Yellowstone Lake from Storm Point.

For less adventuresome keepsakes, check out the park shops, galleries, and museums. Besides the ever-popular T-shirts and mugs, they have a wide range of gifts that evoke the spirit of Yellowstone, including pewter jewelry engraved with images of park wildflowers, locally produced stoneware with park wildlife motifs, items carved from the horns of bison and bighorn sheep or the antlers of elk, Native American crafts, and life-size wood carvings of Yellowstone's wildlife, including eagles, bears, and bison, which range in price $65–300.

The search for other souvenirs became a problem early in Yellowstone's history. That's why people are prohibited from removing just about everything in the park, including plants, animals, rocks, minerals, and archaeological artifacts. Collecting shed elk or deer antlers is big business in Greater Yellowstone, but it's illegal in the park, and violators are charged stiff fines. These regulations are designed to keep Yellowstone intact despite the almost four million visitors per year who want to take a piece of it home.

NOW WHAT?

RRRRRRRRRR

RANGER

70

III.
Getting Around

HIKING TRAILS

WINTER SHUTTLE BUS

MOTORCOACH TOURS

PARKING

BIKE TRAILS

What's the best way to see the park?

There are so many ways to see and enjoy Yellowstone, you might want to take several modes of transportation during your stay. Here's a sampling of what's available.

Driving

Drivers can use nearly 370 miles of paved roads, which pass all of the major attractions and offer many scenic overlooks. A tour and information book titled the *Yellowstone Expedition Guide*, with maps and a CD, can be purchased for $39.99 from Xanterra (307/344-5354, www.travelyellowstone.com). Yellowstone road maps can be downloaded from their website as well. It's always a good idea to call for current road conditions and information (307/344-7381).

Motorcoach Tours

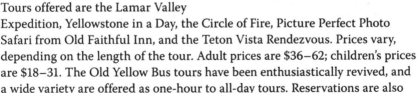

Interpretive Bus/Van tours are available May–September through Xanterra Parks & Resorts (307/344-7311 or 866/439-7375, www.travelyellowstone.com). Tours offered are the Lamar Valley Expedition, Yellowstone in a Day, the Circle of Fire, Picture Perfect Photo Safari from Old Faithful Inn, and the Teton Vista Rendezvous. Prices vary, depending on the length of the tour. Adult prices are $36–62; children's prices are $18–31. The Old Yellow Bus tours have been enthusiastically revived, and a wide variety are offered as one-hour to all-day tours. Reservations are also available through Xanterra.

Gray Line Tours of Jackson Hole and West Yellowstone (800/523-3102; Jackson Hole 307/733-4325; West Yellowstone 406/646-9374; www.graylinejh.com) also gives one-day tours of Yellowstone June–September. The cost is $95 for adults, and children 6–12 are half price.

Bicycling

You can bike the 370 miles of paved roads, a few gravel roads, and 12 bike trails (no backcountry trails or boardwalks), but biking is not exactly for novices. You need to be in good shape and pay close attention to auto traffic because there are no bike lanes or real shoulders along roadways. Between April and June, high snowbanks and narrow winding roads create challenging spring biking conditions. Summer's the best time for riding, but consider riding at dawn to avoid heavy traffic and hot temperatures.

Bicycle rentals, parts, and repairs are available in the towns of Bozeman and Livingston, Montana, north of the park, in West Yellowstone, Montana, at the west entrance; at Jackson, Wyoming, 56 miles south of the park; and at Cody, Wyoming, 53 miles east of the park. Rentals cost $20–25 for a half day and $30–40 for a full day. Check the *Licensed Tour Operators and Outfitters* section of the *Quick Reference* chapter for telephone numbers.

Walking

The best way to escape the crowds and see Yellowstone's backcountry is to walk, hike, or backpack along some of the 1,200 miles of trails within park boundaries. Hikes range from easy walks to see our geothermal features, waterfalls, and lakes to steeper treks  in our remote areas. Assess your limits before setting out on one of these journeys, and remember to bring water, snacks, and extra clothes in case the weather suddenly changes. Read up on backcountry regulations and safety; Yellowstone is bear country. To find out about some great day hikes, take a look at the *Recreational Opportunities* chapter. It's a good idea to stop at the nearest visitor center or ranger station for an update on trail closures and conditions before you start.

Snowmobiling

From December to March, the main mode of transportation is over-snow vehicles on all park roads except the North Entrance Road to the Northeast Entrance, which is plowed for automobiles. You can tour more than 150 miles of groomed roads in a snowmobile with a guide (but not more than 45 miles per hour). Warming huts are located throughout the park and are open 24 hours a day, offering food or just respite from the cold. You can rent snowmobiles and clothing at park gateway communities (Gardiner, Pahaska Teepee, Flagg Ranch, and West Yellowstone) and inside the park at Mammoth Hot Springs and Old Faithful. Fuel, oil, and emergency repair parts are available at Old Faithful, Canyon, and the Mammoth Terraces. Full-day rates run $250 for two riders on one machine, $230 for one rider.

From Mammoth, you can take a full-day guided snowmobile tour to Canyon or Old Faithful for $230 per snowmobile through Xanterra (307/344-7311 or 866/439-7375, www.travelyellowstone.com). You can also contact Xanterra for guided snowmobile rentals.

Cross-Country Skiing and Snowshoeing

From late December to early March, Yellowstone offers backcountry and groomed trails for cross-country skiers and snowshoers of all levels. Ski shops at Mammoth (307/344-5276) and Old Faithful (307/545-4825) offer rentals, instruction, and guided ski tours. Shuttles drop off and pick up skiers at Mammoth and Old Faithful Snow Lodge. Warming huts are located at some road junctions and at Indian Creek. Guided ski tours from Old Faithful and Mammoth give you a chance to explore the Yellowstone wilderness and special points of interest. Contact Xanterra (307/344-7311 or 866/439-7375, www.travelyellowstone.com) for reservations and information.

Snow-Coach Tours

Heated snow-coach tours with short hiking excursions are an easy way to explore the park and view winter wildlife. Tours leave daily from Mammoth, Old Faithful, Flagg Ranch, and West Yellowstone late December–early March. Snow-coach interpretive tours leave from Mammoth Hot Springs three days a week for the Grand Canyon Day tour and the Norris Geyser Basin tour. Contact Xanterra (307/344-7311 or 866/439-7375, www.travel yellowstone.com) for reservations and information.

Horseback Riding

You can saddle up for a one-hour ($36.75) or two-hour ($56.70) guided ride at any of three corrals in the park: Mammoth Hot Springs (mid-May–Aug.), Roosevelt Lodge (mid-June–Aug., and Canyon (late June–Aug.). Contact Xanterra (307/344-7311 or 866/439-7375, www.travelyellowstone.com) for reservations and information. Experienced guides also lead multiple-day horse pack trips into the Yellowstone wilderness.

Special Tours

Wildlife excursions, photo expeditions, historic bus tours, stagecoach rides, boat tours, field courses, and nature study vacations are all available to visitors in Yellowstone.

From May to September, you can join a wildlife excursion to visit our animals' prime natural habitat. Trips depart daily from Lake Hotel, Fishing Bridge RV Park, and Canyon Lodge (adults $45, children $25). Photo expeditions depart from Lake Yellowstone Hotel and Old Faithful (adults $80, children $40). Another option is to take one of the all-day, partial-day, or evening tours with the Historic Yellow Bus Tours. They operate June–mid-September and offer a wide variety of tours from the Circle of Fire to the Teton Vista Rendezvous. The all-day tours are generally $60–80 per seat, and the evening and partial-day tours are $30–50.

From mid-June to September, you can get a dose of the Old West on board a replica of the park's early Concord stagecoach for a rambling 30-minute tour of the Tower-Roosevelt area (adults $13, children 2–11 $8). Rides depart from Roosevelt Lodge. Contact Xanterra (307/344-7311 or 866/439-7375, www.travel yellowstone.com) for reservations.

Between June and September, scenic-cruisers will take you along the northern shore of Yellowstone Lake for one-hour narrated rides that depart from Bridge Bay Marina daily (adults $13, children 2–11 $8). Guided fishing trips leave from Bridge Bay Marina. You can rent your own rowboat, outboard, or dock slip. Contact Xanterra (307/344-7311 or 866/439-7375, www .travelyellowstone.com) for reservations and information. Or enjoy the quiet of Yellowstone or Shoshone Lake on a canoe with a private guide. (See the *Licensed Tour Operators and Outfitters* section of the *Quick Reference* chapter for more information.)

The Yellowstone Association Institute (307/344-2293, www.yellowstone association.org) offers year-round short field courses on the Yellowstone ecosystem. Activities range from classroom presentations to hiking, wildlife-watching, and skiing in the park. Most courses last 2–5 days, and the average tuition is $90–110 per day.

Can we drive our car to most sights in the park?

With 370 miles of paved roadways, which take you near all the main points of interest, Yellowstone can be a motorist's dream (or nightmare when traffic is heavy)—during the months May–October. Once winter really kicks in (by December), all roads are closed until March except the North Entrance Road to the northeast entrance of the park. If you decide to ride in a heated snow-coach or take a brisk outing on a snowmobile, you'll be able to see most of the sights, enhanced by a thick blanket of snow.

Yellowstone Park Service Stations (406/848-7333 or 307/344-2132, www .nps.gov/yell/planyourvisit/gasstatn.htm) operate seven full-service gas stations and four auto towing and repair shops throughout the park. Gas, auto accessories, tire repairs, oil changes, and routine maintenance are available only during the summer. Towing and repair facilities are at Grant Village, Fishing Bridge, Old Faithful Upper, and Canyon Village. You'll find gas stations at Mammoth Hot Springs, Tower Junction, Canyon Village, Fishing Bridge, Grant Village, and Old Faithful Upper and Lower. During the winter, you can get snowmobile fuel at Old Faithful, Fishing Bridge, Canyon Village, and Mammoth Hot Springs.

When driving our narrow roads, you need to be cautious and courteous. Keep an eye out for animals on the road, especially at dusk or night. It's best if you add 30 minutes to any estimate of driving times in the park; that way you won't end up frustrated if you get caught in a buffalo jam or behind a long line of cars. In the winter, be extra careful on icy roads, and remember that the maximum speed inside the park is 45 miles per hour (55 on U.S. 191).

Here are some safety rules to remember:

- Slow-moving vehicles must use pullouts to allow safe passing by other vehicles.
- All vehicles must use pullouts to observe wildlife and scenery.
- Yellowstone has a mandatory front-passenger seat belt requirement.
- It's wise to drive defensively. Remember, our wildlife has the right of way on the roads.

How long does it take to see the entire park?

Although the park covers 2.2 million acres in three states, you could actually drive all the park's roads in about 10 hours. The driving distance between any two developed visitor areas and entrances is never greater than 30 miles. But driving the roads is not really seeing the park. They only offer access to features that deserve a closer look than you can get through your windshield.

In spring and fall, you can probably drive between any two points in an hour or less. In summer, when most visitors come to the park, add at least 30 minutes to account for traffic, road work, and animal jams. Your Yellowstone experience will be more complete when you get out of your car, take a nature walk, and drop by our visitor centers to learn about the natural wonders that surround you. To glimpse just the main features in the park, we suggest that you stay in the park at least three days. Get up before dawn one or two mornings, and drive to an overlook in the Hayden, Antelope Creek, or Lamar Valley. You may be lucky enough to see a grizzly bear or a wolf pack.

The more time you spend in the park, the more you'll be able to see and appreciate: Yellowstone wildlife (best seen at dawn and dusk); the park's thermal features (whose eruptions may take some patience to see); the vast scenic beauty of our valleys; waterfalls and canyons; Yellowstone, Lewis, and Shoshone Lakes; and the solitude available if you are willing to walk half a mile from the road.

On your left... the majestic moose silhouetted against the Washburn mountains...

Where can we buy buffalo jam and what exactly is it?

You don't buy buffalo jam—you run into it. And although it can make your travel in Yellowstone a little sticky, it's not really jam. The phrase actually refers to a traffic jam, Yellowstone style. A buffalo jam can be anything from an entire herd of migrating elk to a single, stubborn bison in the middle of the road. Regardless of what animal it is, believe me, they have the right of way.

When the bison, elk, bear, coyote, and others use the roads as an extension of their grazing grounds, the result is something like the rush hour you might experience on city freeways. As a result, you might want to allow at least 30 extra minutes when driving in the park. Although our animals are very unpredictable, there are certain areas where you can usually expect traffic to slow or come to a complete halt for the animals, including the roads around Old Faithful, the Lamar and Hayden Valleys, and certain areas around Lake Yellowstone.

If you're caught in one of our jams—be it buffalo, elk, bear, or coyote—it's important that you remember our buffalo jam guidelines.

- If you want to stop, pull out in one of the designated parking areas along the road.

- If traffic looks like it will be stopped for a while and you want to get out of your car, don't forget to close your car doors to make passage by other cars and people easier.

- Most importantly, don't go any closer than 100 yards to the animals, especially bear.

And remember: Relax, it's probably the most enjoyable and picturesque traffic jam you'll ever experience.

Can we take a walk with a ranger?

Most ranger-led walks are scheduled from the first half of June through early September, but check at any visitor center or look through your copy of *Yellowstone Today* (www.nps.gov/yell/planyourvisit/yellowstone-today .htm). Look for ranger-led programs online at www.nps.gov/yell to find out about early or late season activities, as well as starting dates and times. The following sampling of the activities will give you an idea of the range of subjects covered; schedules and topics change slightly from year to year.

CANYON AREA
Hayden Valley Venture
Learn who Hayden was and how the valley was formed, and get a chance to see local wildlife. Half-day hike on Fridays.

Rim Reflections
Explore the geology and natural history of the Yellowstone River, its Grand Canyon, and its majestic waterfalls. Meet at Uncle Tom's Trail parking area on the road to Artist Point. 1–2 hours, daily.

Beyond the Rim
Walk along the upper Grand Canyon of the Yellowstone River. 2.5 hours, daily.

GRANT VILLAGE/WEST THUMB AREA
Hot Water Wilderness
Explore the origins of geysers, mud pots, and hot springs. Meet at West Thumb Visitor Information Center. 1.5 hours, daily.

Tracking Yellowstone's Wildlife
Understand animal signs, read the forest. Meet at West Thumb Visitor Center. 1 hour, daily.

LAKE VILLAGE AND FISHING BRIDGE AREA
Yellowstone Lake Reflections
Walk through meadow, through forest, and along lakeshore to learn more about the largest high-elevation lake in North America. Meet at Indian Pond, three miles east of Fishing Bridge. 2 hours, daily.

MADISON AND WEST YELLOWSTONE AREA
Evening Program on Yellowstone's Wonders
Topics for these talks vary. Meet at the Madison Amphitheater. 45 minutes, daily.

Explore Yellowstone!
Rangers offer suggestions on how to best use your time. Meet at the West Yellowstone Visitor Information Center. 30 minutes, daily.

MAMMOTH AREA
Mammoth Hot Springs Terraces
Trace the park's colorful geologic history along the terraces. Meet at Liberty Cap Rock Formation, at the base of the hot springs. Moderately strenuous. 1–2 hours, daily.

Touring Historic Fort Yellowstone
Take a short evening walk to learn about the army's role in the formation of the park. Meet in front of the Albright Visitor Center. 1 hour, daily.

NORRIS AREA
Norris Geyser Basin
Learn secrets about the park's hottest, most dynamic, and oldest geyser basin. Meet at the Norris Geyser Basin Museum. Bring water and sunglasses. 1.5 hours, daily.

OLD FAITHFUL AREA
Geyser Hill Walk
Take a one-mile walk through the greatest concentration of geysers on earth. Meet at Old Faithful Temporary Visitor Center. 1.5 hours, daily.

Geyser Geology Walk
Take a 1.5-mile walk through the Upper Geyser Basin, and explore the rarest geological features on earth. Meet at Castle Geyser, a 15-minute walk west of the visitor center. 1.5 hours, daily.

Sunset Geyser Basin Walk
Take a leisurely one-mile sunset walk through the Upper Geyser Basin to learn more about the dynamic yet fragile nature of geysers. Meet at Castle Geyser, a 15-minute walk west of the visitor center. 1.5 hours, daily.

Are there any self-guided tours of Yellowstone?

There are eight self-guided trails to help you learn more about park history, geyser basins, geology, wildlife, scenery, and forest fires. Armed with 50-cent trail guide booklets, you can tour the following points of interest at your own pace.

Mammoth Hot Springs Terraces
Meander along a walking trail through the Lower Terraces, and take a one-way drive through the Upper Terraces to see wonderful views of these fascinating formations. Pick up the trail guide in the parking area in front of Liberty Cap at the base of the terraces.

Fort Yellowstone Walking Tour
Take a short walk around old Fort Yellowstone at Mammoth Hot Springs to learn more about the human history of the park. Many of the structures in the Fort Yellowstone historic district are employee houses, so please respect the privacy of residents by staying on the paved route. Pick up the trail guide in front of the Albright Visitor Center.

Upper Geyser Basin
Tour the greatest collection of geysers in the world, including Old Faithful. Several miles of trail and boardwalk begin at the Old Faithful Visitor Center, where you can pick up a trail guide. Stop by the center for orientation and information on the geyser eruptions.

Grand Canyon of the Yellowstone
View the canyon and Upper and Lower Falls from roadside overlooks along the rim drives. North Rim Drive takes you to Inspiration, Grandview, and Lookout Points, and a spur road goes to an overlook at the brink of Upper Falls. South Rim Drive leads to Uncle Tom's Trail and Artist Point. Trails also wind along both rims.

Pick up the trail guide at Canyon Visitor Center, where there's a great exhibit on the park's geology; at the dispenser at Inspiration Point; or at the brink of the Upper Falls trailhead.

Norris Geyser Basin

Explore the hottest, most active thermal basin in Yellowstone on several trails that start at the parking lot. You can pick up a trail guide in front of the visitor center.

Fountain Paint Pots

See active, ever-changing mud pots on a trail eight miles north of Old Faithful on the road to Madison Junction. You'll find a trail guide at the parking lot.

Mud Volcano

See intriguing and explosive mud pots with appropriate names, such as Dragon's Mouth, six miles north of Fishing Bridge Junction. Pick up a trail guide at the start of the boardwalk.

West Thumb Geyser Basin

Follow a boardwalk past colorful boiling springs next to icy waters on the west shore of Yellowstone Lake. You can also view West Thumb, a steam explosion crater. The trail guide is at the parking lot.

Calcite Springs Overlook and Tower Falls

Look down on Calcite Springs and see unusual geological formations in the northernmost area of the Grand Canyon of the Yellowstone, 1.5 miles south of Tower Junction. A short trail 2.6 miles south of Tower Junction leads from a parking lot past the store to an overlook of the 132-foot waterfall.

Fire Trails

See the effects of fire on park forests along the Children's Fire Trail, six miles east of Mammoth Hot Springs on the Mammoth-Tower Road. The trail was built by children and educational groups after the fires of 1988. Another short, accessible fire trail, Two Ribbons Trail, winds through burned forest along the Madison River, about five miles east of the west entrance.

You can also stop by any of the Yellowstone visitor centers to purchase a variety of trail guides and leaflets, travel maps, and auto tour CDs. To prepare for your trip, you can purchase items from the Yellowstone Association bookstore (www.yellowstoneassociation.org).

YELLOWSTONE'S UNIQUE WILDLIFE AND GEOLOGY

- Yellowstone National Park has the largest concentration of free-roaming wildlife in the lower 48 states and the global temperate zone. Populations include:

  7 species of native ungulates (hoofed animals)

  2 species of bears

  64 species of other mammals (approximate)

  299 species of birds

  18 species of fish (5 non-native)

  7 species of reptiles

  6 species of amphibians

  5 species protected as "threatened or endangered:"

  grizzly bear

  gray wolf

  whooping crane

  bald eagle (delisted in 2007)

  peregrine falcon (delisted in 1999)

- The park contains at least 60 percent of the world's geysers, the largest and most diverse collection in existence.

- The park contains one of the world's largest calderas, measuring 1,316 square miles, or 28 miles by 47 miles.

Are there any guided trips into Yellowstone's backcountry?

Yellowstone Association Institute (307/344-2293, www.yellowstoneassociation.org) offers winter and summer backcountry courses. You can also visit Yellowstone's backcountry with a private outfitter. Make sure the outfitter you choose has a permit from the National Park Service, because those companies offer professional guides with a keen understanding of Yellowstone history, geography, and ecology. For a complete list of registered park guides, see the *Licensed Tour Operators and Outfitters* section of the *Quick Reference* chapter.

Be aware that a journey into Yellowstone's backcountry isn't exactly a "walk in the park." You need to be in good shape and know your ability to tackle these adventures. Here are a few wilderness trips you might want to try:

Canoe or kayak trips on Lewis, Shoshone, and Yellowstone Lakes allow quiet exploration of backcountry areas filled with abundant wildlife and breathtaking scenery, far away from roads and human habitats. Jackson Hole Kayak School (307/733-2471, www.jacksonholekayak.com) offers multiple-day canoe/kayak and camping trips depart in July and August, with costs ranging $250–305 a day (meals and equipment included), depending on the number of participants and the length of the trip.

You can travel Yellowstone's wilderness by saddle horse. Scenic horse pack trips take you into remote areas of the park, where you can cast your line into some of the country's best fishing spots, photograph vast wild landscapes, or simply gaze upon our soul-soothing, high-country scenery. Horse pack trips through John Henry Lee Outfitters (307/733-9441 or 800/352-2576, www.johnhenrylee.com) accommodate all riding levels and needs.

Guided day fishing trips are another way to reach the park's finest fishing holes, including those on the Yellowstone, Madison, and Firehole Rivers, Lewis and Yellowstone Lakes, and many smaller streams. Try Jack Dennis Fishing Trips (307/733-3270, www.jackdennis.com) or Westbank Anglers (307/733-6483 or 800/922-3474, www.westbank.com).

Is there a shuttle in Yellowstone?

Well...yes and no...

There's no shuttle service March–November. From mid-December to March 1, we have several shuttles to transport skiers to and from some of the best skiing trails in the park. Contact Xanterra (307/344-7311) for more information and reservations for any of these shuttles.

There's a free daily shuttle from the Mammoth Hot Springs Hotel to the Mammoth Terraces Ski Trail and the Mammoth Snowmobile Hut, which connects snowmobilers in Mammoth with the park's snow-road system. The shuttles run every half hour 7:30 A.M.–5 P.M., and on-call service is available 24 hours a day.

Another shuttle from the Mammoth Hotel takes skiers to cross-country ski trails on the Blacktail Plateau, Lost Lake, Tower Falls, and the Chittenden Loop. The shuttle runs daily 8:30 A.M.–4:30 P.M. at a round-trip cost of $11 for adults and $5.50 for children. Reservations are required. (Be prepared: Temperatures in the Tower-Roosevelt area can be 10–30°F lower than at Mammoth.)

Daily snow-coach shuttles also drop off and pick up at Mammoth Hot Springs Hotel, Golden Gate, and Indian Creek in the Mammoth Area 8:30 A.M.–3:45 P.M. Round-trip fare is $14.50 for adults and $7.25 for children. Reservations are required. (Hint: Temperatures at Indian Creek can be 10°F lower than at Mammoth, and often wind makes the area even colder).

Snow-coach shuttles from the Old Faithful Snow Lodge drop off skiers at Fairy Falls or the Continental Divide for some of the best trails in the Old Faithful area. Drop-off fare is one-way $13.50 for adults and $6.75 for children. No pickups are available. Reservations are required.

Ski/snowshoe drops are also available one-way from West Yellowstone to Seven-Mile Bridge for $15 or Madison Junction for $30.

Where are the best spots and best times to take pictures?

Whether you're capturing wildflower blooms or the sheer grandeur of Lower Falls, a memorable photograph of Yellowstone awaits at every turn. The quality of light will bring these pictures to life, and every hour of the day offers a different shade.

The mood of light cast upon the park's waterfalls changes dramatically in the course of a day. All the falls can be best photographed on overcast days when there's adequate but diffused light. During bright summer days, rich colors are found in the early morning or late afternoon. Try to capture Upper and Lower Falls from Artist Point 8–9 A.M., or walk along the South Rim Trail between Artist Point and Uncle Tom's Trail.

Other great photo opportunities await on an early morning or evening walk to Storm Point, about three miles east of Fishing Bridge, where you can watch the sun rise and fall over Yellowstone Lake. Early risers and late afternoon hikers also have a good chance of taking pictures of our wildlife in their natural habitat, such as bison, moose, marmots, and waterfowl around the lake. Just remember to stay at least 25 yards from larger animals and at least 100 yards from bears.

How about a shot of Mammoth Terraces as the golden sun rises behind Mount Everts, illuminating the clouds of steam and water dripping from the terraces? Maybe you'll be lucky enough to see elk roaming the area. A walk through the geyser basins might give you a photographer's dream shot of one of the park's most amazing features.

The fun part is finding your own perfect scene to capture on film, from the burned whitebark pines of Mount Washburn to a secret backcountry trail. Photo walks led by Kodak photographers are offered during the summer. (Check *Yellowstone Today* for schedules and locations.) You can buy film at gift shops in our lodging facilities, Xanterra gift shops, and photo shops throughout the park. For those who can't wait to see the results, one-hour processing is available at Canyon Village, Old Faithful, Grant Village, and Fishing Bridge.

How does winter change getting around in the park?

The truth is, winter changes just about every aspect of getting around the park. Park roads are restricted to snowmobiles and snow-coaches, except for the North Entrance Road to the Northeast Entrance, which is plowed for automobiles. For hikers, a great way to see our backcountry is to switch to cross-country skis or snowshoes.

Guided snow-coach tours into the park depart daily from Old Faithful, Mammoth Hot Springs, West Yellowstone, and the South Entrance. Sightseeing tours on ski shuttles, snow-coaches, snowmobiles, snowshoes, and cross-country skis are offered daily from Old Faithful and Mammoth Hot Springs, beginning around mid-December.

You can rent skis and other equipment at ski shops, which are open for the season at Mammoth and Old Faithful or in Gardiner and West Yellowstone. Check at the front desk of Old Faithful Snow Lodge or Mammoth Hot Springs Hotel for shuttle schedules to and from ski trails (see the *Where can we ski in the park?* section of the *Recreational Opportunities* chapter). They can also give you maps of all the local ski trails. Snowmobile fuel is available at Mammoth, Old Faithful, Canyon, Fishing Bridge, and gateway communities outside the park.

Warming huts located throughout the park help visitors pry off winter's icy fingers with a toasty room and a hot drink. Wildlife pay heed to winter's changes as well; they're often found roaming the groomed roadways, especially around Mammoth and the Geyser Basins. This means that snowmobilers have to pay special attention, because vehicles must give the right-of-way to animals at all times.

IV.
Lodging
and
Dining

Where can we stay in the park?

A fter a day of wildlife-watching or geyser gazing, a shower and a comfortable bed can be a great way to end the day. From May through October, you can choose among 2,200 overnight accommodations in nine lodgings inside the park. From December to early March you can pick from 360 rooms at the Old Faithful Snow Lodge and cabins or Mammoth Hot Springs Hotel. Year-round, rooms range from rustic cabins without baths to suites in the hotels. Remember, most park roads close late October–December and again early March–mid-April. Snow permitting, some roads open to over-snow travel mid-December–early March. For updates, check www.nps.gov/yell/planyourvisit/hours.htm. For the latest park road information contact the National Park Service (307/344-7381). For reservations at any of Yellowstone's nine lodgings, contact Xanterra Parks and Resorts (P.O. Box 165, Yellowstone National Park, Wyoming 82190, 307/344-7311 or 866/439-7375, www.travelyellowstone.com). Dinner reservations are also made through Xanterra. Make room reservation six months in advance for the summer season.

Please note that all park accommodations are nonsmoking. To reflect the natural surroundings of Yellowstone, televisions, radios, air-conditioning, and Internet hook-ups are not available. Wheelchair accessible accommodations are available on a limited basis.

In 1903–1904, the **Old Faithful Inn** was built in Yellowstone as a work of art designed to complement the natural beauty of the Upper Geyser Basin landscape. Today it is a National Historic Landmark. It boasts a soaring lobby ceiling with overhanging balconies made from local timbers and a huge fireplace made from 500 tons of local stone. Today it has 327 rooms, ranging from suites for $457 to rooms without bath for about $91. There are free daily 40-minute walking tours of the inn. For information, stop by the inn's activity desk.

First opened in 1891, **Lake Yellowstone Hotel** was restored to its 1920s grandeur in 1990. The hotel combines a white-columned front porch, a large sunroom with spectacular views of Yellowstone Lake, and original wicker furniture that evokes the casual western elegance of another era. It's listed on the National Register of Historic Places and is the lodging of choice for visiting dignitaries. Its 292 accommodations range in price from $525 for a suite to around $139 for a standard room with bath. Frontier cabins include baths and cost around $110.

Built in 1936, the **Mammoth Hot Springs Hotel** is named for the steaming limestone terraces just above the hotel. It offers a choice of 97 rooms, from suites for $356 to rooms without baths for about $82. It also has 116 cabins (available May–October), ranging from cabins with hot tubs for around $182 to Frontier cabins for $104 to cabins without baths for $72. From December to March prices range from $339 for a hotel suite to $78 for a room without bath. No cabins are available in the winter, but you can rent the hot tubs in the Frontier cabins by the hour. Winter Getaway Value Packages are available and must be booked by phone through Xanterra. Package rates are valid from the beginning of January to early March. Packages may include guided wildlife tours via skis or snowmobile, tours between Old Faithful and Mammoth, breakfasts, ice skating, hot tub rental, and discount snow cards valid for gift shop purchases, ski rentals, and additional meals.

Following a dramatic increase in the number of visitors driving cars in the early 1900s, the Yellowstone Park Camping Company built three rustic lodges to provide simple overnight accommodations for the wave of tourism. **Roosevelt Lodge** was built in 1920 near Teddy Roosevelt's favorite camping site close to Tower Falls. The cabins still welcome visitors with western hospitality, family-style dining, and rustic lodging. Available June–September, cabins with bath run $104, and Roughrider cabins with wood-burning stoves and no baths go for around $64.

Old Faithful Lodge Cabins saw conversion from an old camp into a lobby, recreation hall, office, and shops. There are 132 cabins total, some with baths ($104) and some without baths ($67). The lobby and food court (with cafeteria and bakery) feature commanding views of Old Faithful.

The **Lake Lodge and Cabins** boast a log lodge, a lobby with two fireplaces, a large porch overlooking Yellowstone Lake, and cozy cabins that create a family-friendly atmosphere. Large cabins with bath are $132, and Pioneer cabins with bath go for about $65.

The original Canyon Hotel, built in 1910–1911, was replaced in 1957 by the new **Canyon Lodge and Cabins,** near the Lower Falls and the Grand Canyon of the Yellowstone. New lodge rooms run just over $155, and cabins with baths range $66–142.

At **Grant Village,** 300 comfortable motel-style units sit in view of Yellowstone Lake with easy access to the park's south entrance and Grand Teton National Park. The village is named after President Ulysses S. Grant, who signed the bill to establish Yellowstone as a national park in 1872. Rooms with baths range $125–130.

Year-round accommodations at the **Old Faithful Snow Lodge and Cabins** include 100 guest rooms in a facility that was renovated in 1999. It is the newest of the park's full service hotels and has been recognized with the

Cody Award for Western Design and *Travel and Leisure*'s Inn of the Month. It offers a full service dining room, a quick service grill (The Geyser Grill), and a gift shop. During the months May–October, prices range from $184 for a lodge room with bath to $91 for a Frontier cabin with bath, with comparable rates during winter.

If you bring your own room in the form of a recreational vehicle, you can reserve space at the **Fishing Bridge RV Park** from the middle of May to the end of September. There are 344 sites with full hookups only for hard-sided vehicles with a maximum length of 40 feet. Sites are back-in only, no pull-through. Cost per space is $35 per night. Contact Xanterra Hotels and Resorts, (307/344-7311 or 866/439-7375, www.travelyellowstone.com) to reserve space—at least six months in advance.

There are 11 campgrounds in Yellowstone. Four of these, Bridge Bay Campground, Canyon Campground, Madison Campground, and Fishing Bridge RV Park, have more than 1,400 individual campsites and can be reserved through Xanterra's Yellowstone Reservation Center (307/344-7311 or 866/439-7375). The remaining seven campgrounds are available on a first-come, first-serve basis. Mammoth Campground is operated by the NPS and is open year-round.

If you're in the park and haven't made reservations, you can always check with the lodging desks about last-minute cancellations. Although visitors do cancel from time to time, this is not a recommended way to find a place to stay in the park, especially during our summer season.

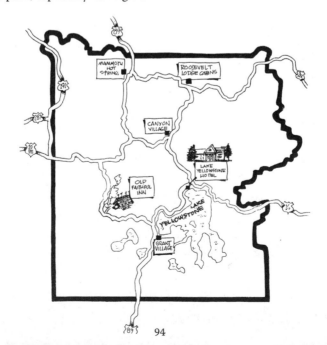

Are there convenient places to stay just outside Yellowstone?

No matter what direction you're coming from or what time of year, there are lots of places to stay just outside the park's five entrances, and here are some of them. Most prices listed range from low-season single-occupancy to high-season double-occupancy rates. Lodgings are open year-round, unless otherwise noted. For nearby chambers of commerce, which can supply listings of more lodgings, see the *Telephone Directory* section of the *Quick Reference* chapter.

Highway 89 from the North

Pray, Montana, 34 Miles from the north entrance:

Chico Hot Springs Resort $39–345
406/333-4933 or 800/468-9232   151 units
www.chicohotsprings.com
Full service resort with hot springs, gourmet dining, convention center, horseback riding, dog sledding, complete day spa. National register of historic places since June 1999.

Gardiner, Montana, within 5 miles of the north entrance:

Absaroka Lodge $45–115
406/848-7414 or 800/755-7414   41 units
www.yellowstonemotel.com
All rooms have balconies on the Yellowstone River.

Best Western Motel   rooms $75–160, suites $150–250
406/848-7311 or 800/828-9080   85 units
www.bestwestern.com
Pool, sauna, some kitchenettes, cable TV, air-conditioning, public laundry.

Jim Bridger Court Cabins $69–100
406/848-7371 or 888/858-7508   18 cabins
Clean but rustic individual cabins, picnic area, pets allowed. Open May–October only.

Yellowstone Village Inn rooms $59–159, condos $129–219
406/848-7417 or 800/228-8158 43 units
www.yellowstonevinn.com
Continental breakfast, pool, sauna, satellite TV, wireless Internet.

Highway 20 from the West
West Yellowstone, Montana, near the west entrance:
Prices are based on double occupancy high season rates and are subject to change.

Gray Wolf Inn and Suites rooms $59–169, suites $79–319
800/852-8602 102 units
www.graywolf-inn.com
pool, hot tub, sauna, wireless Internet, parking garage.

Hibernation Station $119–299
406/646-4200 or 800/580-3557 50 cabins
www.hibernationstation.com
Kitchenettes, suites, log furniture, tapestry walls, fireplaces, hot tub. Pets accepted.

Holiday Inn Sunspree Resort $99–399
406/646-7365 123 units
www.doyellowstone.com
Indoor pool and whirlpool, WI-FI, restaurant and saloon

Yellowstone Inn $80–150
406/646-7633 or 800/858-9224 10 units
www.yellowstoneinn.net
Air-conditioning, microwaves, refrigerators. Pets accepted.

Yellowstone Park Inn and Suites $59–179
406/646-7681 84 units
www.westyellowstonemotels.com
Restaurant and outdoor pool.

Highway 89 from the South
Flagg Ranch, Wyoming, 2 miles from the south entrance:

Flagg Ranch Resort $165–175
800/443-2311 92 cabins
www.flaggranch.com
Coffee, patios in forest setting. Tent camping spaces available.

Grand Teton National Park, Wyoming, 20 miles from the south entrance:

Jackson Lake Lodge rooms $189–269, suites $450–625
800/628-9988 385 units
www.gtlc.com/lodgeJac.aspx
Closed winter.

Highway 20 from the East

Cody, Wyoming, 52 miles from the east entrance:

Best Western Sunset	rooms $50–169, suites $89–215
Hwy. 20	12 units
307/587-4265	
www.bestwestern.com	
Indoor/outdoor pool, hot tub.	

Cody Budget Host	$52–107
307/587-4258	24 units
Family units available.	

Lockhart Bed and Breakfast Inn	$79–115
307/587-6074	13 units
www.stayincody.com	
Historic house overlooking Shoshone River, full breakfast.	
RV camping spaces available.	

Skyline Motor Inn	$39–99
307/587-4201	46 units
www.skylinemotorinn.com	

Highway 212 from the Northeast

Cooke City, Montana, 4 miles from the northeast entrance:

Alpine Motel	$69–140
406/838-2262 or 888/838-1190	27 units
www.cookecityalpine.com	

Elkhorn Lodge	rooms $64–84,
406/838-2332	cabins with kitchenettes $99
www.elkhornlodgemt.com	8 units

High Country Motel	rooms $60–90, cabins $70–90
406/838-2272	15 units
www.cookecityhighcountry.com	
Some cabins with kitchens and fireplaces.	

Hoosier's Motel	$75–90
406/838-2241	12 units
Closed winter.	

Silver Gate, Montana, 1 mile from the northeast entrance:

Silver Gate Lodging	cabins $75–165
406/838-2371	25 units
www.pineedgecabins.com	

Where can we eat in the park?

Yellowstone offers a full range of dining and snacking (www.nps.gov/yell/planyourvisit/wheretoeat.htm), from historic dining rooms to casual cafeterias, fast-food joints, delis, and fountain shops. Kids get their own menus, casual clothing is always acceptable, and all eating areas are nonsmoking. Four dining rooms in the park require advance reservations: Grant Village, Lake Hotel, Mammoth Hotel, and Old Faithful Inn. See the *Telephone and Website Directory* section in the *Quick Reference* chapter for numbers.

The fanciest evening meals in Yellowstone are served daily in the dining rooms at Mammoth Hot Springs Hotel, Old Faithful Inn, Grant Village, Canyon Lodge, and Lake Hotel. Menus include prime rib, steak, seafood, chicken, and vegetarian entrées and daily specials with prices that won't break the bank. Full-service breakfast and lunch are also served. You must make advance reservations, except at Canyon Lodge. Guests without reservations often have a long wait.

For casual dining, try the Lake House Restaurant in Grant Village, where dinner entrées include pasta and pizza selections. It also serves breakfast with a lake view. Check out the restaurant at Roosevelt Lodge for barbecued ribs in an old-west atmosphere. Also try the Old Faithful Snow Lodge. It has reasonable prices and a family-style atmosphere.

If quick-and-easy eating is your goal, try one of the park's three cafeterias, located at Lake Lodge, Old Faithful Lodge, and Canyon Lodge. Entrées and à la carte selections include salads, sandwiches, pasta, chicken, and prime rib. A full breakfast menu is available at Lake Lodge and Canyon Lodge, and all three cafeterias are open for lunch and dinner.

Fast-food options are found throughout the park. Try breakfast, lunch, or dinner at the Terrace Grill at Mammoth Hot Springs or the Pony Express at the Old Faithful Inn. The Four Seasons Snack Shop near the Old Faithful Snow Lodge has fast-food lunches and dinners, and the deli at the Lake Hotel has made-to-order sandwiches, soups, and other quick fixes. Snack shops at Old Faithful Lodge, Lake Lodge, and Grant Village serve quick eats and fountain drinks, and the fountains in the Yellowstone General Stores at Old Faithful, Canyon, Grant, Lake, and Tower Falls serve hamburgers and sandwiches. One of my favorite breakfast haunts is the fountain at the Old Faithful Yellowstone General Store.

If you have a hankering for sweets, you can pick up an ice cream, frozen yogurt, cookie, or beverage at the snack shops in Old Faithful and Canyon Lodges, the Terrace Grill, Pony Express, and Four Seasons Snack Shop. Grocery areas in the Yellowstone General Stores at Old Faithful, Mammoth, Canyon, Fishing Bridge, Lake, and Grant also carry a slew of snacks, sweet and savory.

Lounges offering drinks and light snacks are located in most lodging facilities, including Old Faithful Inn, Mammoth Hot Springs Hotel, Grant Village, Canyon Lodge, Lake Hotel, Lake Lodge, and Roosevelt Lodge.

For a dining experience that is pure Yellowstone, board an old-fashioned wagon or ride horseback from Roosevelt Lodge to an Old West Dinner Cookout in Pleasant Valley. It's a feast: steak, corn, coleslaw, cornbread muffins, homemade Roosevelt beans, watermelon, apple crisp, and more. The cost is $53 per adult and $43 per child 4–11 years old. Contact Xanterra Parks & Resorts, (307/344-7311 or 866/439-7375, www.travelyellowstone.com) for reservations and rates for horse rides. This is a popular activity and tends to book up fast—especially the horseback ride.

WE'RE HUNGRY!!

What about dining in one of the nearby towns?

PRAY, MONTANA
30 miles from the north entrance:

The Chico Inn at Chico Hot Springs
406/333-4933
Excellent menu and atmosphere; a little pricey but worth it! Try the Poolside Grill for more casual—and moderately priced—fare.

GARDINER, MONTANA
Next to the north entrance:

Sawtooth Deli and Restaurant
406/848-7600
Full breakfast menu with burritos and huevos rancheros. Daily specials, deli subs and sandwiches, barbecue specialties, and wood-fired brick oven pizzas. Dinner menu has pastas, seafood, steaks, and more, all at reasonable prices.

Town Café
406/848-7322
Family cooking at reasonable prices. Breakfast, lunch, dinner served with loft steakhouse restaurant upstairs.

Yellowstone Mine Restaurant
406/848-7336
Dinner here features fine dining such as steaks, prime rib, seafood, pasta, salads, nightly Chef's Special, appetizers, and specialty desserts. Full bar available. A reasonably priced breakfast is also served, and a breakfast buffet is available in the summer months.

WEST YELLOWSTONE, MONTANA
Next to the west entrance:

Running Bear Pancake House
406/646-7703
Family restaurant specializing in pancakes, but also has great burgers, salads, sandwiches, and bakery goods at moderate prices.

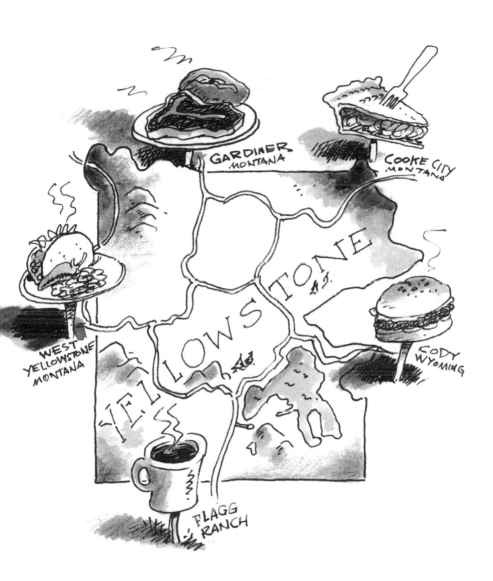

GARDINER
MONTANA

COOKE CITY
MONTANA

WEST
YELLOWSTONE
MONTANA

CODY
WYOMING

YELLOWSTONE

FLAGG
RANCH

Sydney's Mountain Bistro
406/646-7660
Full fine dining menu at moderate prices.

Three Bear Restaurant
406/646-7811
www.threebearlodge.com
Down-home cooking featuring prime rib, steaks, and chicken at moderate prices. Take out available.

TJ's Bettola (on Airport Road)
406/646-4700
Italian food, steaks, and seafood at moderate prices.

GRAND TETON NATIONAL PARK
20 miles from the south entrance:

The Mural Room, Jackson Lake Lodge
307/543-2811
Unparalleled scenery, great breakfast buffet, excellent dinner menu, if a bit pricey.

Pioneer Grill, Jackson Lake Lodge
307/543-2811
Good food and casual fountain atmosphere, with reasonable to moderate prices.

The Peaks Restaurant and The Trapper Grill, Signal Mountain Lodge
307/543-2569
Good food at reasonable prices.

CODY, WYOMING
52 miles from the east entrance:

Eugene's
307/587-2989
The nightly smorgasbord is a good deal and popular with families.

La Comida
307/587-9556
Good Mexican cuisine at reasonable prices.

RJ's Café
307/527-4420
Good breakfast and lunch place with reasonable prices.

Silver Dollar Bar and Grill
307/587-3554
Serving up the best hamburgers in town—and reasonable prices, too—in a cowboy atmosphere.

The Pollard
406/446-0001
The Pollard is a historic hotel with an elegant dining room and oak-paneled public rooms. Serves breakfast and dinner.

COOKE CITY, MONTANA
4 miles from the northeast entrance:

Beartooth Café
406/838-2475
Tasty selection of burgers and sandwiches at reasonable prices.

The Bistro
406/838-2160

Buns N Beds
406/838-2030

SILVER GATE, MONTANA
1 mile from the northeast entrance:

Log Cabin Café and Bed and Breakfast
406/838-2367

Where can we pick up picnic supplies?

With nearly 50 established picnic areas along the way to some of the park's major features, Yellowstone is the ultimate picnic spot. Where you decide to spread your tablecloth is up to you, but here are your choices for stocking up on goods.

If you don't want to do the fixing, you can order a box lunch from any dining room or cafeteria. Place your order the night before by calling 307/344-7901, and it will be ready to pick up in the morning. You get a sandwich with your choice of smoked turkey, roast beef, pastrami, or ham with cheese, a piece of fruit, a drink, and cookies. Vegetarian lunches are also available.

For sandwiches and drinks made to order or to go, you have lots of options, including the Lake Yellowstone Hotel Deli, the Four Seasons Snack Shop near the Old Faithful Snow Lodge, the Terrace Grill at Mammoth Hot Springs, and the Pony Express in the Old Faithful Inn. Light snack food can be purchased from the soda fountains at Canyon, Old Faithful, Lake, and Grant Village. You can also order sandwiches and drinks to go from the fountains at the Yellowstone General Stores in Old Faithful, Canyon, Grant Village, Lake, and Tower.

Other good sources for picnic supplies are the grocery aisles of the Yellowstone General Stores located in Old Faithful, Mammoth Hot Springs, Canyon, Fishing Bridge, Lake, and Grant Village. Or you can shop for groceries in all the gateway communities around the park.

You can enjoy live music at two places in the park. The Mammoth Hot Springs Hotel often features soothing piano music in its Map Room in the late afternoon. It's quite a treat to relax in the lounge sipping an espresso and watching the elk graze outside while listening to your favorite tunes. Beginning in January, the hotel offers live entertainment each weekend, with a variety of contemporary music. Ask the front desk for a schedule of piano performances.

The Sun Room at the Lake Hotel is a great place to listen to piano or chamber music while you enjoy a drink before supper and relish spectacular views of the lake. To find out more about these concerts, stop by the hotel.

Are there any special seasonal events in and around Yellowstone?

You bet. When it comes to celebrating special occasions in the park, all roads seem to lead to park headquarters at Mammoth. From the year-round sumptuous Sunday breakfast buffets to the great New Year's Eve Dinner Dance and the Valentine's Day Dinner, Mammoth is definitely where it's happening.

To bring a little color to the white quilt of winter, Mammoth hosts several specialty buffets, including a Mexican Fiesta, Italian Night, a Specialty Chocolate Buffet, and a Western Barbecue. For more information on these and other events, contact Xanterra Parks & Resorts (307/344-7311 or 866/439-7375, www.travelyellowstone.com).

You'll also find interesting special events in the Greater Yellowstone Area. The town of Jackson, Wyoming, hosts Old West Days (307/733-3316) during the third week of May, with walking historical tours of downtown Jackson, a rodeo, street dances, parades, concerts, and Native American dancers. That same week, the Mountain Man Rendezvous (307/739-2753), taking place in Teton Village, down Highway 89 from Jackson, revives Yellowstone's bygone era of trappers and hunters, with authentic trapper events, tepee villages, and muzzle-loader shooting contests.

Over the Fourth of July, Stampede Days (307/587-2297) in Cody, Wyoming boast a world-class rodeo and other events celebrating the cowboy heritage. During July and August, you can listen to classical and contemporary music in the Jackson Hole area at the Grand Teton Music Festival (www .gtmf.org). Teton Village hosts concerts, open rehearsals, and young people's programs. During the third week in September, you'll have a chance to view the best paintings, photographs, and multimedia images of our national parks, historic sites, and monuments, when Jackson Lake Lodge exhibits the top 100 entries in the Arts for the Parks national competition.

Cross-country skiers from all over the U.S. and Europe gather each Thanksgiving week in West Yellowstone for training and coaching on the area's early snow (www.yellowstoneskifestival.com). Fifty kilometers of trails groomed to perfection offer a long season of superb skiing (www.rendezvous skitrails.com). In March, join in the 50km, 25km, or shorter races (www .rendezvousrace.com). Ski rentals and lessons are available from Freeheel and Wheel (406/646-7744, www.freeheelandwheel.com).

OLD FAITHFUL INN FACTS

- The Old Faithful Inn opened for visitors in 1904. It contained 140 rooms and was described as the largest log hotel in existence. The total cost of the original building was less than $100,000.

- The primary building materials for the original hotel were all native to the Yellowstone area: The logs were gathered from local forests; the stone, including 500 tons required for the fireplace, was quarried from a hill about five miles from the site, on the road to West Thumb; the entrance doors were made of split logs; and all hardware, including the clock on the front of the fireplace, was hand wrought by a local blacksmith.

- The massive, rough-stone fireplace is actually eight fireplaces combined into one structure. The central lobby measures 64 feet square and rises to 76.5 feet at the ridge.

- The architect, Robert C. Reamer, also designed other structures in Yellowstone, including:

   An addition to and remodel of Lake Yellowstone Hotel

   Canyon Hotel (destroyed by fire in 1960)

   The Roosevelt Arch at the north entrance to the park

   Last remodel of the Mammoth Hotel

- The original Old Faithful Inn building has been expanded and remodeled several times. In 1913, the East Wing was built, adding 100 rooms. The West Wing, with 150 rooms, was constructed in 1928. With various changes over the years to the interior layout of the hotel and its public spaces, the inn today has a total of 330 guest rooms.

- The Old Faithful Inn is listed on the National Register of Historic Landmarks.

V
Camping and Backpacking

Be careful out there.

What types of campgrounds are available in Yellowstone?

Of the park's dozen campgrounds, the National Park Service (307/344-7381, www.nps.gov/yell/planyourvisit/camping-in-yellowstone.htm) runs seven: Indian Creek, Lewis Lake, Mammoth, Norris, Pebble Creek, Slough Creek, and Tower Falls. These campgrounds, with a total of 454 sites, range in size from Slough Creek's 29 sites to Norris's 116. They are available on a first-come, first-served basis. Parking is limited, but you do get drinking water, toilets (flush or vault), fire grills, and picnic tables. Fees are $12 per night for all except Mammoth and Norris, which are $14 per night. Yellowstone Park (www.yellowstonepark.com/PlanYourTrip/CampingInfo.aspx) also provides up-to-date information about camping in the park.

The other five campgrounds in the park are located near the main visitor areas, at Bridge Bay, Canyon, Grant Village, Madison, and Fishing Bridge RV Park. With a total of 1,750 sites, these are our largest campgrounds, ranging from 272 sites at Canyon to 432 at Bridge Bay. Sites can be reserved in advance through Xanterra Parks and Resorts (advance reservations 307/344-7311 or 866/439-7375, same-day reservations 307/344-7901). Fees are $17 except for Fishing Bridge RV Park, which costs $37 for 1–4 people.

Bridge Bay Campground is located near Yellowstone Lake, adjacent to the Bridge Bay Marina, boat launch, and store. The camp has a sanitary dump station but no utility hookups. Pay showers and a coin laundry are within four miles. Canyon Campground, close to the Grand Canyon of the Yellowstone, has stores, restaurants, pay showers, a coin laundry, but no utility hookups. Grant Village Campground is located along the southwestern shore of Yellowstone Lake. Within a half mile you'll find stores, restaurants, pay showers, a coin laundry, and a sanitary dump station, but no utility hookups. Madison Campground is centrally located just 14 miles east of the west entrance and 16 miles north of Old Faithful, near where the Gibbon and Firehole Rivers join to form the Madison River. It offers a sanitary dump station but has no utility hookups or showers. Fishing Bridge RV Park is near the northwest shore of Yellowstone Lake and offers full hookups (hard-sided units only, maximum length 40 feet). Fishing Bridge has a coin laundry, pay

showers, a store, electricity, water, sewer hookups, and a sanitary dump station, but no fire grates or picnic tables.

All the park campgrounds are listed below with helpful information, but here are some quick facts: Campgrounds are generally open from May or early June through September, with Madison, Lewis Lake, and Slough Creek closing later, around November 1. Mammoth is the only campground open year-round. Pay showers and coin laundries are located in or near Bridge Bay, Canyon, Grant Village, and Fishing Bridge. Amenities for disabled campers are available at Bridge Bay, Canyon, Grant Village, and Madison. Senior Pass and Access Pass holders are given a 50 percent discount on camping fees everywhere but Fishing Bridge RV Park. Group camping areas, located at Madison, Grant, and Bridge Bay Campgrounds, are available for large organized groups with a designated leader. The group camps are open late May–early November, and fees range $49–79 per night, depending on the size of the group. Remember, camping is allowed only in designated areas for your safety.

CAMPGROUNDS IN YELLOWSTONE

Campground	No. of Sites	Approx. Dates**	Fee	Elev. (ft)	Toilets	Showers/ Laundry Nearby	Dump Station	Generators Permitted (8 A.M.–8 P.M.)
Bridge Bay*	432	5/25–9/16	$17	7,800	Flush		X	X
Canyon*	272	6/8–9/9	$17	8,000	Flush	X		X
Grant Village*	425	6/21–9/23	$17	7,800	Flush	X	X	X
Madison*	277	5/4–10/28	$17	6,800	Flush		X	X
Mammoth	85	year-round	$14	6,200	Flush			X
Norris	116	5/18–9/24	$14	7,500	Flush			X
Indian Creek	75	6/8–9/17	$12	7,300	Vault			
Lewis Lake	85	6/15–11/4	$12	7,800	Vault			
Pebble Creek	32	6/8–9/24	$12	6,900	Vault			
Slough Creek	29	5/25–10/31	$12	6,250	Vault			
Tower Falls	32	5/18–9/24	$12	6,600	Vault			
Fishing Bridge RV*	344	5/18–9/30	$37	7,800	Flush	X	Sewer	X

*Reserve through Xanterra Parks & Resorts (307/344-7311 or 866/439-7375)

** Dates are approximate and may depend on weather or resource management concerns.

What are the campgrounds outside Yellowstone

If you arrive late and without reservations, you still have camping options, so don't just head for home. The Greater Yellowstone Area has lots of campgrounds in pleasant locations close to park entrances. Many are near great hiking trails in national forests surrounding the park.

National forest service campgrounds (877/444-6777, www.recreation.gov) have developed sites with drinking water, tables, fire pits or grills, toilets, and garbage containers. Fees usually range $7–15 per night, and you'll pay a little extra for more than one vehicle per site. Only a few of the larger campgrounds can accommodate small trailers and motor homes, so call ahead to make sure. If you're driving a big rig, be warned that there are no electrical hookups or dumping facilities for RVs in any of the national forest campgrounds.

Another option is to find an informal, undeveloped site anywhere in the national forests, except in areas posted for no camping or for day use only. Many of these sites are located along short spur roads that branch off forest roads and highways. Or they may be just parking places, with only enough room for your vehicle. When you use one of these undeveloped sites, don't forget to carry out all your trash, use extra caution with campfires, and observe the same rules as if you were inside the park. (See the *Are there any limits or restrictions on camping?* section of this chapter.)

The first national forest campgrounds to fill up in the high season (July and August) are the ones closest to park entrances in scenic locations. These usually include campgrounds between Cody, Wyoming, and the east entrance to the park, those along the Beartooth Highway near the northeast entrance at Cooke City/Silver Gate, Montana, and the ones near West Yellowstone, Montana. You need to arrive at these popular campgrounds as early in the day as possible to get the best sites. Most fill by late afternoon or early evening in peak season. Some sites can be reserved in advance.

The chart on the following pages gives more detailed information on a selection of national forest campgrounds surrounding the park, campgrounds located in Grand Teton National Park, and private campgrounds in close proximity to the park. Use the numbers below to make advance reservations or for more information on any of these campgrounds.

NEAR WEST ENTRANCE
Gallatin National Forest
(also near the north and northeast entrances)
Hebgen Lake Ranger District
406/823-6961

Gardiner Ranger District
406/848-7375

Targhee National Forest
Island Park Ranger District
208/558-7301

Yellowstone Grizzly RV Park
4 blocks from the west entrance
406/646-4466, www.grizzlyrv.com
Tent sites $29.95/day, RV $44.95–54.95

Madison Arm Resort
near West Yellowstone
406/646-9328, www.madisonarmresort.com

NEAR NORTH ENTRANCE
Rocky Mountain Campground
Gardiner, MT
877/534-6931

NEAR SOUTH ENTRANCE
Bridger-Teton National Forest
Buffalo Ranger District/Blackrock Ranger Station
307/543-2386

Flagg Ranch Resort and Campground
John D. Rockefeller Memorial Parkway, 2 miles from the south entrance
800/443-2311, www.flaggranch.com

Grand Teton National Park
307/739-3603 for recorded information on site availability

Colter Bay Campground
800/628-9988

NEAR EAST ENTRANCE
Shoshone National Forest (also near the northeast entrance)
North Zone Ranger District
307/527-6921

Campgrounds Outside Yellowstone

Campground	Location	No. of Sites	Approx. Dates*	Max. Trailer Length (ft.)	Facilities
Near West Entrance:					
Beaver Creek	Gallatin	79	6/10-9/10	32	tb, tl, w, b, f
Cabin Creek	Gallatin	15	5/15-9/15	32	tb, tl, w, f
Cherry Creek	Gallatin	6	5/31-10/15	no limit	tb, tl
Spring Creek	Gallatin	10	5/31-10/15	no limit	tb, tl, fa
Lonesomehurst	Gallatin	27	5/15-9/15	32	tb, tl, w, f, bl, te, fa
Box Canyon	Targhee	17	5/31-9/10	25	tb, tl, w, f, fa
Buffalo	Targhee	105	5/31-9/10	32	tb, tl, w, f, b, pr, fa, ra
Upper Coffeepot	Targhee	14	5/31-9/10	25	tb, tl, w, f, b, fa
Flat Rock	Targhee	38	5/31-9/10	25-35	tb, tl, w, f, b, fa
Yellowstone Grizzly RV Park	West Yellowstone	181	5/8-10/15	45-80	full-service resort
Madison Arm	West Yellowstone	96	5/15-10/1	40	full-service resort
Near North Entrance:					
Tom Miner	Gallatin	16	6/1-10/31	40	tb, tl, w, f, b
Rocky Mountain	Gardiner, MT	87	4/15-10/15	45	full-service resort
Near South Entrance:					
Sheffield Creek	Bridger-Teton	5	5/20-9/30	no limit	tb, tl, f, b
Turpin Meadow	Bridger-Teton	18	5/20-9/30	25	tb, tl, w, f, b, fa
Hatchet	Bridger-Teton	9	5/20-9/30	25	tb, tl, w, f, b
Flagg Ranch	Rockefeller Mem. Pkwy.	147	5/25-9/23	no limit	full-service resort
Lizard Creek	Grand Teton NP	60	6/6-9/2	30	tb, tl, w, f, fa
Colter Bay	Grand Teton NP	350	5/25-9/23	no limit	tb, tl, w, f, bl, te, s, l, pr, fa, RV

Campground	Park/Forest	Sites	Dates*	Max	Facilities
Colter Bay RV Park	Grand Teton NP	112	5/15-9/30	no limit	tb, tl, w, f, bl, te, s, l, pr, fa, RV
Signal Mountain	Grand Teton NP	81	5/5-10/19	30	tb, tl, w, f, te, pr, fa, bl, RV
Near East Entrance:					
Big Game	Shoshone	17	6/15-9/30	32	tb, tl, w, f, b, pr, fa
Wapiti	Shoshone	42	5/25-9/30	50	tb, tl, w, f, b, pr, fa
Elk Fork	Shoshone	13	5/1-9/30	22	tb, tl, w, f, b, pr
Clearwater	Shoshone	20	6/15-9/30	40	tb, tl, w, f, b, fa
Rex Hale	Shoshone	30	5/25-9/30	40	tb, tl, w, f, b, pr, fa
Newton Creek	Shoshone	31	5/1-9/30	22	tb, tl, w, f, b, fa
Eagle Creek	Shoshone	20	5/25-9/30	22	tb, tl, w, f, b, fa, no tents
Three Mile	Shoshone	33	5/25-9/30	32	tb, tl, w, f, fa, no tents or pop-up trailers
Near Northeast Entrance:					
Soda Butte	Gallatin	27	7/1-9/30	48	tb, tl, w, f, b
Colter	Gallatin	23	7/15-9/30	48	tb, tl, w, f, b
Chief Joseph	Gallatin	6	7/15-9/30	42	tb, tl, w, f, b
Fox Creek**	Shoshone	27	6/5-9/30	32	tb, tl, w, f, b, fa
Crazy Creek	Shoshone	19	6/1-10/20	32	tb, tl, w, f, b, fa
Lake Creek	Shoshone	6	7/1-9/7	22	tb, tl, w, f, b, fa
Hunter Peak	Shoshone	9	6/1-11/30	32	tb, tl, w, f, b, fa
Beartooth Lake	Shoshone	21	7/1-9/7	32	tb, tl, w, f, b, bl, fa
Island Lake	Shoshone	20	7/1-9/7	32	tb, tl, w, f, b, bl, fa

*Opening dates subject to change based on weather and other conditions.
**To reopen after upgrade for 2009 camping season.

Key:

tb	tables	w	water
tl	toilets	f	firepits or grills
s	showers	b	bear-resistant containers
l	laundry	bl	boat launch
te	telephones		
pr	paved access roads		
fa	fishing access		
RV	sanitary dump stations		

Can we make reservations for a campground?

Five of the campgrounds in the park take reservations: Bridge Bay, Canyon, Grant Village, Madison, and Fishing Bridge RV Park. To reserve a site at any of these, contact Xanterra Parks & Resorts (P.O. Box 165, Yellowstone National Park, WY 82190, advance reservations 307/344-7311 or 866/439-7353, same-day reservations 307/344-7901) as early in advance as you can.

For group campsites, advance reservations are required. You can make them beginning January 1 by contacting Xanterra Parks & Resorts. The only advice I can give you on the first-come, first-served campgrounds at Mammoth, Norris, Indian Creek, Lewis Lake, Pebble Creek, Slough Creek, and Tower Falls is *arrive early.* During our peak camping season (early July–late August), these campsites fill up by early morning. So get to the campground of your choice as early as possible to secure a site.

Although most of the campsites in the national forests just outside Yellowstone's five entrances are on a first-come, first-served basis, some can be reserved in advance. Refer to *What are the campgrounds outside Yellowstone?* section of this chapter for the telephone numbers. All the campgrounds in Grand Teton National Park close to the south entrance to Yellowstone are available on a first-come, first-served basis, with the sites at Signal Mountain filling by 10 A.M., at Colter Bay by noon, and at Lizard Creek by 2 P.M. during the peak season. So plan to do your sightseeing after you've secured one of these sites. It's best to reserve campsites in advance at Flagg Ranch, which is just two miles from the south entrance to the park. For a larger sampling of the private campgrounds in or near the gateway communities, call the Chamber of Commerce numbers listed in the *Telephone and Website Directory* section of the *Quick Reference* chapter.

Are there any limits or restrictions on camping?

Although you may be tempted to spend the entire summer in one of our campgrounds, we do have limits. You can camp for up to two weeks June 15–September 15 and up to a month the rest of the year, except at Fishing Bridge RV Park where you can stay as long as you like. The maximum size for RVs in the park is 40 feet long. For limits at all other campgrounds surrounding Yellowstone, check the chart following the *What are the campgrounds outside Yellowstone?* section of this chapter.

And Now for the Rules:

- Camping or sleeping in vehicles is permitted only in designated campsites inside the park. However, camping in undeveloped sites is allowed on national forest lands surrounding Yellowstone.

- A maximum of six people (unless you're a family with more than four dependent children) may occupy a campsite.

- Group camping is available at Madison, Grant, and Bridge Bay Campgrounds for large organized groups with a designated leader. Advance reservations are required.

- Pets are allowed in our campgrounds late spring–late fall, but they must be leashed at all times. They're not allowed in any area more than 25 feet from campgrounds, roads, or parking areas, and they're not allowed on trails, in buildings, on boardwalks, or in the backcountry unless they're service/assistance dogs for people with disabilities. Pets may not be left alone at a campsite.

- Quiet hours are 8 P.M.–8 A.M. in all campgrounds except Bridge Bay RV Park where the hours are 10 P.M.–7 A.M.

- Food must be stored in bear-proof lockers where those are provided. No food should be left open in your vehicle.

- You can only run a generator 8 A.M.–8 P.M.

- Dishwater and sewage must be discarded in designated utility drains.

- You aren't permitted to connect electrical extension cords to restroom outlets.

Well, we got that out of the way.
Now, let's go camping!

Hmmm...

Can we build a campfire?

The comforting crackle of a campfire is one of the best parts of camping, but campfires have caused some of our forest fires. Follow a few guidelines, so that our next generation of campers can enjoy fireside gatherings as well.

Start by only using established fire pits, then check around the area for potential spark hazards. Never leave a fire unattended; put it out by stirring in water before you leave the campground, and do a final check for any remaining embers. Fires are allowed in most established campgrounds but are discouraged in backcountry areas. There, small fires are permitted only in existing fire rings at specific campsites. To protect our wilderness environment, backpackers are asked to use small portable stoves for cooking and boiling water.

Use only dead and down wood or purchased firewood for fires. Wood is sold in some of the campgrounds, including Indian Creek, Mammoth, Norris, Madison, Bridge Bay RV Park, Grant, and Canyon. The gathering of firewood is becoming an issue in Yellowstone's popular camping areas, where natural processes cannot supply dead wood fast enough to feed campfires during our summer season. Do not break, cut, or saw branches from any standing tree, dead or alive. It's best if you use only small sticks and branches for your fire. These will burn completely, so you won't have to deal with partially burned logs. If you try to break or saw branches from trees in Yellowstone, you could end up with a hefty $50–100 citation.

PUTT
PUTT
PUTT

Are there any special activities around the campgrounds that we should know about?

Starting in early June and running through Labor Day, park naturalists present a variety of programs in all areas of the park, from guided walks to geology and history field talks to evening slide presentations and campfire programs exploring varied subjects. Here are some recent topics: "The National Park Idea," "The Greater Yellowstone Ecosystem," "The History of Yellowstone," "The Issues of Yellowstone," "Wildlife," "Geology," and "The Aquatic World of the Park."

Evening campfire programs are presented nightly at Mammoth, Norris, Madison, Old Faithful, Grant, Bridge Bay, Fishing Bridge, and Canyon; three times a week at Lewis Lake; twice a week at Tower Falls; and once a week at Pebble Creek. To find out about times and locations, check your copy of *Yellowstone Today*, ask at the visitor center nearest your campground, or look at the ranger-naturalist program listings at each campground.

After sunset, the temperature drops fast, and it gets really dark, so come prepared with rain gear, warm clothes, and flashlights.

Here's a sampling of some of the areas and subjects covered by the ranger-naturalists on some of the guided walks:

Hayden Valley Walk; Walking the Canyon Rim; Lakeshore Geologic Discovery at West Thumb; Geyser Basin; Summer of Fire Mud Volcano Exploration; Yellowstone Lake Reflections; Managing the Wild in Roosevelt Tower area; Evening Stroll in the Madison Area; Mammoth Hot Springs: The Lower Terraces; The Army Years: Touring Historic Fort Yellowstone; Norris Geyser Basin Walk; Hellroaring Trail in the Tower/Roosevelt Area; Lost Lake Trail; Northern Yellowstone Geyser Hill Walk near Old Faithful Geyser; Geology Walk; and Sunset Geyser Basin Walk.

Keep in mind that these programs change from time to time—check the park website (www.nps.gov/yell) for a current list.

Where can we rent camping gear and buy supplies inside the park?

You'll need to rent gear before you arrive or in the gateway cities surrounding the park. You can rent (or buy) gear at sporting goods stores east of the park in Cody, Wyoming; north of the park in Bozeman, Livingston, and Gardiner, Montana; south of the park in Jackson, Wyoming; and west of the park in West Yellowstone, Montana. Once you're inside the park, there just isn't any place to rent gear.

If you have a tent, you can buy almost any other camping gear in one of the Yellowstone General Stores inside the park. Good-quality sleeping bags and companion sleeping pads are readily available in a variety of types and prices. Backpacks and camping stoves of all types and for a variety fuels are available. You'll also find plenty of camping lanterns, enamel camp ware as well as inexpensive plastic cutlery. It's best to call ahead to check on inventory at the particular store before you arrive. For store telephone numbers, see the *Telephone and Website Directory* section in the *Quick Reference* chapter.

You can buy propane fuel at the Fishing Bridge and Grant Village Service Stations from mid-May to late September or early October. Food supplies can be purchased at stores throughout the park.

Wherever you get your camping gear, make sure you have a tent with rainfly, ground cloth, warm sleeping bag, sleeping pad, flashlight, extra socks, food, cooking stove and fuel, pot, spoon, cup, water bottle, and any personal gear.

Do we need to make reservations for backcountry campsites?

Yellowstone has a system of designated backcountry campsites. Of the approximately 300 backcountry sites inside the park, most are reservable in advance. Since the demand for campsites in our backcountry often exceeds the supply, I would advise you to make advance reservations.

We've made the process as painless as possible: You can request a Backcountry Trip Planner, including a reservation form and maps showing all campsite locations, from the Central Backcountry Office (P.O. Box 168, Yellowstone National Park, WY, 82190, 307/344-2160 or 307/344-2163, www .nps.gov/yell/planyourvisit/backcountryhiking.htm). Use this form to submit your advance reservation by mail, or you can submit it in person no more than 48 hours in advance of your trip—in which case there's no reservation fee. Telephone and fax reservations are not accepted.

We begin booking reservations for backcountry campsites on April 1 of the current year. You're welcome to send your reservation request in before that date, but that won't guarantee you'll be at the top of the list. On April 1, all requests in hand are randomly prioritized and processed.

Each individual-trip advance reservation costs $20 (regardless of the number of nights or number of people involved). Submit the fee with your Trip Planning Worksheet request. We accept cash, money orders, travelers checks, or personal checks (payable to the National Park Service). Once your reservation has been entered into the computer, this fee cannot be refunded. You'll receive a confirmation notice, which you then exchange at one of the nine backcountry offices in the park for the actual backcountry use permit that you will need for all backcountry camping.

There must be some mistake. We have a reservation for this site...

Are there any organized trips into Yellowstone's backcountry?

We offer lots of opportunities to explore our many backcountry areas year-round with the help of a guide.

From late spring to fall, Xanterra Parks & Resorts offers one- and two-hour guided trail rides through the valleys and canyons around Mammoth Hot Springs, Canyon Village, and Roosevelt Lodge. Xanterra also offers guided fishing trips on cabin cruisers on Yellowstone Lake June–September. Photo safaris leave from the Old Faithful Inn between June and the end of September. You can also join a late-afternoon wildlife excursion in the Lamar Valley. Although you won't go into the backcountry, you may see bison, elk, pronghorn, bears, and wolves. Excursions depart from Canyon, Bridge Bay, Lake Yellowstone Hotel, and Fishing Bridge RV Park. To make reservations, check current prices, and to get information for all of these trips, contact Xanterra Parks and Resorts (307/344-7311 or 866/439-7375, www.travel yellowstone.com).

The Yellowstone Association Institute (P.O. Box 117, Yellowstone National Park, WY 82190, 307/344-2293, www.yellowstoneassociation.org) offers backpacking and horse trips into some of our backcountry areas as part of its annual courses. Contact the Yellowstone Institute for a catalog of courses that will give you detailed information on the trips, dates, and prices.

In the winter, you can tour some of the park's most beautiful backcountry areas on guided ski tours that depart daily from Mammoth Hot Springs

and Old Faithful. From Mammoth you can explore the Grand Canyon of the Yellowstone or follow a guide on an all-day ski tour to Cooke City. Snowshoe tours depart from Old Faithful. Custom guided snowmobile tours are available, but they're expensive. Contact Xanterra Parks & Resorts (307/344-7311 or 866/439-7375, www.travelyellowstone.com) for schedule information, reservations, prices, and to find out about custom tours.

If you want to immerse yourself thoroughly in the Yellowstone wilderness, your best bet is to join one of the many wilderness outfitters and companies who are registered to lead guided trips into the park. They offer backpacking, fishing, biking, canoeing or kayaking, day hiking, and photography adventures, as well as horse or llama trips. Outfitters also offer trips into the national forests around the park. Prices vary with the length of trip, number of people, and services provided. For a complete list of currently registered outfitters and wilderness companies, see the *Licensed Tour Operators and Outfitters* section of the *Quick Reference* chapter or consult the National Park Service website (www.nps.gov/yell/planyourvisit/stockbusn.htm).

When and why do we need backcountry use permits?

Backcountry use permits are required for overnight stays in backcountry areas. They're free and are available daily 8 A.M.–4:30 P.M. at the ranger stations and visitor centers listed below. These permits help to avoid over-crowding during peak season, provide important safety information, and help rangers keep track of hikers and campers. You generally don't need a permit for day hiking, but it's best to check on trail conditions with a ranger station, ask at a visitor center, or call the Central Backcountry Office (307/344-2160 or 307/344-2163).

You must obtain a backcountry use permit in person, not more than 48 hours before your first camping date. When you get your permit, you'll choose specific campsites for each night of your trip, unless you've already reserved in advance. Because most campsites are one-party sites, you'll have them to yourself. Most of our sites can accommodate 8–12 campers maximum, although some can host larger groups. Pick up your permit at a park ranger station before 10 A.M. on the day you start your backcountry trip; otherwise, you might lose your spot. If certain campsites and/or trails are closed for safe-ty or resource protection, we'll help reroute your trip as close as possible to your original request. For any questions, call the Central Backcountry Office.

For the best information, get your permit from the ranger station or visi-tor center closest to where your trip begins. Pickup locations are: Canyon Ranger Station or Visitor Center; Mammoth Ranger Station or Visitor Center; Old Faithful Ranger Station; Tower Ranger Station; West Entrance Ranger

Why don't **you** have to apply for these permits?

124

Station; Grant Village Backcountry Office; South Entrance Ranger Station; and Bechler Ranger Station.

Permits can sometimes be obtained from the East Entrance Ranger Station when a ranger is available to help you. However, these rangers have other duties and may not be available at all times.

Ranger station and visitor center hours may vary during spring, fall, and winter. To obtain a backcountry permit during these seasons, call the main park number (307/344-7381).

Fire in Yellowstone

- Long before people and modern firefighting came to Yellowstone, lightning caused most fires in the area. By studying fire scars on old trees, we can tell that the higher forests in Yellowstone were swept by a major blaze every 200–400 years, and about every 25 years fires spread across the lower grasslands around Gardiner and along the North Fork of the Shoshone River newar Cody. These fires were eventually extinguished by nature through rainstorms or snowfalls, or they extinguished themselves by running into a river or stream, a wet meadow, or a different type or age of forest.

- Wildfires are as important to Yellowstone's ecology as sun, wind, rain, and snow.

- Before 1988, the last major fires in the Greater Yellowstone Ecosystem were in 1750 and 1850, and some parts of the park hadn't burned for 300–400 years. Extremely dry weather, high winds (60 miles per hour), high temperatures, a large buildup of dead material on the forest floor, and 2,000 lightning strike in one day combined to ignite, fuel, and spread the huge fires of 1988 (248 of them). Once again, it was nature in the form of snowfalls in September that finally extinguished the flames, with help from the largest firefighting effort in U.S. history.

- Although the impact of the 1988 and 1994 fires was great – 800,000 acres in 1988 and 16,350 acres in 1994 together blackened nearly half the area of the park – the forest floor is once again showing vigorous new growth and creating new ecological possibilities. Elk now graze on nutrient-rich regrowth, snags provide nesting cavities for birds such as woodpeckers and bluebirds, and vibrant flowers, such as fireweed, grow from the ash-fed soil.

- If you want to learn more about fire's effect on nature in Yellowstone, visit the exhibit at the Grant Visitor Center.

When is the best time of year to visit Yellowstone's backcountry?

When you're planning a backcountry trip, keep in mind that most of the trails in Yellowstone are over 7,000 feet above sea level. This means that many areas are under snow until June or even mid-July. And in the spring and early summer, some of our creeks and streams swell to 25 feet wide, are extremely cold, and run swiftly 3–6 feet deep, making crossings problematic. On a map you can't tell whether a stream is a raging torrent or just a swollen creek. Here's a list of when some of the backcountry areas in the park are generally free of snow or standing water and can be reached safely. But keep in mind that I've based this on historical information, which may change from year to year. To find out if a route is open or advisable, call the Central Backcountry Office (307/344-2160 or 307/344-2163), or talk to a ranger who is familiar with the area.

Early May: Yellowstone River Trail near Gardiner, although Hellroaring Creek is too swift and deep to ford until mid-August.

Mid- to late May: Upper and Lower Cache Creek; Upper Daly Creek; Slough Creek.

Early June: Gardiner River area; Coyote Creek; Imperial Meadows; Sentinel Meadows; Lone Star; Upper Firehole; Firehole Springs.

Mid- to late June: Straight Creek South; Mount Holmes; Black Butte Creek; Gallatin River area; Fan Creek; Cascade, Grebe, and Ribbon Lakes; Pebble Creek; Seven-Mile Hole; most of Shoshone Lake (although some access could be dangerous); some of Yellowstone Lake; Thorofare Trail from Nine-Mile Post to Beaverdam Creek; Mallard Lake; and most Old Faithful sites.

Early July: Sportsman Lake from west side; Wolf Lake; Lamar River to Mist Pass; Bliss Pass; Thunderer; Heart Lake; Union Falls in Bechler area.

Mid- to late July: Agate Creek; Crescent, Shelf, and High Lakes; Fawn and Bighorn passes; Sportsman Lake from east side; Electric and Bighorn Peaks; Moss Creek; Observation Peak; Specimen Ridge; Hoodoo Basin; all Yellowstone Lake sites; Mountain Creek to Thorofare; some Snake River and Basin Creek sites; Two-Ocean Plateau; Bechler and Lower Fords; Dunanda Falls in Bechler area.

August: Wapiti Lake; Thorofare to park boundary; Trail Creek; Eagle Pass; Bechler River Canyon; Pitchstone Plateau; Snake River; Basin Creek; Summit Lake.

127

What should we know about camping and backpacking in Yellowstone's backcountry?

A wilderness excursion requires more preparation than a walk around Old Faithful. Check with the nearest ranger station or visitor center for current weather and trail conditions before you set out, and be prepared in case the forecast is completely wrong.

You can reserve a campsite in advance for a $20 fee. Otherwise, you'll be assigned a campsite of your choice from the available sites when you pick up your free backcountry use permit at a ranger station or visitor center no more than 48 hours before your camping date. Most campsites are for a maximum of 8–12 people; a few are set aside for larger and smaller groups.

Campfires are allowed only in established fire pits, using only dead and down wood. Attend to your fire at all times, and extinguish it before you leave. Backpacking stoves are allowed at all campsites and are useful for sites that don't allow ground fires or wood fires.

Bury human waste 6–8 inches deep and a minimum of 100 feet from any watercourse. Discard wastewater at least 100 feet from a watercourse or campsite. Don't pollute lakes, ponds, rivers, or streams by using them to wash your body, clothing, or dishes.

Horses, burros, mules, ponies, and llamas may be used as pack animals, but because of their size, they can damage fragile areas. Using animals means you're responsible for minimizing the signs of their passing. You're not permitted to use stock overnight before July 1, due to range readiness and/or wet trail conditions, and you can't bring horses into front country campgrounds. For a list of licensed outfitters who provide guided backcountry trips using stock, see the *Licensed Tour Operators and Outfitters* section of the *Quick Reference* chapter, or consult the National Park Service website (www.nps.gov/yell/planyourvisit/stockbusn.htm).

You must carry out of the backcountry all refuse, including items partly burned in fire pits (foil, tin, glass, etc.). Remember to select a tent site that's 100 yards from your food preparation area, free of tree hazards, and not visible from trails, other campsites, and lakeshores. If possible, do not trench around your tent or level the site. Before you start, plan your meals carefully, and package your food in reusable containers or plastic bags to reduce the amount of trash.

The following are not allowed in the backcountry: firearms, pets, motorized equipment, and wheeled vehicles. Removing, defacing, or destroying any plant, animal, or mineral is prohibited. Leave historical and archaeological items in place, and report all findings of these items to a park ranger.

For your safety, here are a few important guidelines:

- Leave a note detailing your travel plans with a reliable person. Stick to the route and camp where you planned, so rangers will know where to look if they need to find you.

- Purify all drinking water by boiling it 3–5 minutes or using Giardia-rated filters or iodine-based chemical treatments.

- To avoid hypothermia, stay dry, stay out of the wind, and avoid getting chilled. Put on rain gear before you get wet, warm clothes before you get cold. Wear a hat, vest, and gloves to conserve your body heat. Keep fueled by eating and drinking. Watch for symptoms: uncontrolled shivering, slow speech, exhaustion, and memory lapses. Treatments include putting on dry clothing, bundling into a warm sleeping bag, and drinking warm, sweet (nonalcoholic) liquids.

- If you wish, pick edible plants, berries, and mushrooms for your daily consumption, but if you don't know which ones are edible don't eat them.

- Be very cautious in backcountry thermal areas. They may have thin, fragile crusts. Don't travel in these areas after dark. Swimming, bathing, or soaking in thermal water is prohibited.

- Remember that grassy, low-elevation areas (4,000–6,500 feet) are prime tick habitat mid-March–mid-July. Wear repellent, tuck pants into boots, tuck shirts into pants, and check your body frequently. Mosquitoes are widespread in summer, especially around wet areas. Repellents and heavy clothing provide the best protection.

- Use extreme caution crossing rivers before July 1 and after summer rainstorms. The water is cold, fast, and dangerous. Do not ford

barefooted, and use a long sturdy stick for balance. If you're crossing with a group, lock arms or hold hands. Search for the safest and shallowest place to cross—you don't have to cross where trail meets stream. Undo the waist and chest straps of your pack, so you can shed it quickly if you fall.

• If possible, bring a topo map and compass, and know how to use them. Maps can be ordered from the Yellowstone Association (P.O. Box 117, Yellowstone National Park, WY 82190, 307/344-2293, www.yellowstone association.org). Contact the Central Backcountry Office (307/344-2160 or 307/344-2163, www.nps.gov/yell/planyourvisit/backcountrytripplanner.htm) to get your backcountry trip planner, which gives lots of useful information.

See also the *Backcountry Regulations* section of the *Quick Reference* chapter.

What is Yellowstone's backcountry wilderness like?

It's really wild!

Since less than two percent of the total area of Yellowstone National Park is developed, about 98 percent is wilderness—with an emphasis on wild. We have more free-roaming wildlife than anyplace in the lower 48 states, and some of the wildest weather too. So be prepared for weather and trail conditions that change quickly and for possible encounters with animal residents.

The backcountry offers one thing year-round: unpredictability. At elevations of 7,000–11,000 feet, your dusty trail can turn into a muddy path faster than you can say "Did we pack rain gear?" In spring and summer, the winter runoff can transform streams and rivers into torrents of wild water, so cross carefully. In winter, when you swap your boots for snowshoes and cross-country skis, a peaceful snowfall can escalate into a whiteout or blizzard.

The more than 300 backcountry campsites are located throughout the park's 2.2 million acres. These sites offer few amenities: a fire ring, a food pole, and an occasional bear-resistant container, at most. For more information on the wilderness areas and campsites, call the Central Backcountry Office (307/344-2160 or 307/344-2163).

Here's a sampling of what you'll find in the park's backcountry regions:

The northwest corner of the park is filled with low valleys and steep ridges, offering spectacular views of the forested hills, mountain peaks, streams, and lakes. Elk and deer roam the high ridges in summer and the river valleys in spring and fall. Moose feed along the willow-lined streams, and bighorn sheep live on the slopes and ridges near Sheep Mountain and Bighorn Peak. Grizzly bears and a wolf pack also frequent this area.

The park's northern area around the Gallatin Mountains and Mammoth boasts one of the highest peaks (Electric Peak) and alpine meadows in Yellowstone. The area is home to many of the park's large mammals—moose along streams, a herd of bighorn sheep on Quadrant Mountain, and elk that summer throughout the Gallatin Mountains and migrate to the lower slopes and valleys in winter. Grizzly and black bears hunt on the ridges and in the valleys.

In the Lower Yellowstone River and Tower region you can see Specimen Ridge's petrified forest, Hellroaring Mountain and its 2,000-foot block of granitic rock, and a lively mix of trees, such as Douglas-fir, aspen, cottonwood, limber pine, and Rocky Mountain juniper. Because in winter the snow is shallower here than elsewhere, the area attracts bison and elk. Pronghorn and mule deer winter near Gardiner. Bighorn sheep forage on windblown ridges, and coyotes follow wolves around for leftovers. In summer, deer and pronghorn return, and you may see an occasional black bear.

Lamar River, Slough Creek, Pebble Creek, and Soda Butte Creek all drain the rugged Absaroka Range of the park's northeast corner. After late July, the snow leaves the mountain passes, the mosquitoes thin out in the forests, and the streams recede and become easier to cross. The Lamar Valley is the main winter range for the northern Yellowstone elk herd and a herd of bison, and it is also home territory for several packs of gray wolves.

Pelican Valley includes the headwaters of Pelican and Broad Creeks. Here you'll find broad meadows, backcountry lakes and thermal features, and forested land that was burned in the fires of 1981, 1988, and 1994. This area, especially Pelican Valley, is prime grizzly bear habitat and is strictly off-limits to any hiking until July 4 each year. Then it's open daily 9 A.M.–7 P.M., but no off-trail travel is permitted along the first 2.5 miles of the Pelican Valley Trail.

The Canyon area of the park is dominated by the Grand Canyon of the Yellowstone. The trails in the area either provide striking views of the canyon and its waterfalls or take you through varying terrain, from forested lakes to large open meadows and even to the top of Mount Washburn. Bighorn sheep, mule deer, elk, moose, bison, and grizzly bears frequent the area.

The Central Plateau contains Nez Perce and Hayden Valleys and the plateau, which was near the center of one of the largest volcanic eruptions on the face of the earth. The resulting volcanic soil supports extensive lodgepole pine forests. Hayden Valley, a remnant of an older Yellowstone Lake, produces a rich array of plant life that attracts pocket gophers, grizzly bears, and bison.

Approaching the Old Faithful area from the west via the Madison Valley, you travel past the steep-walled canyon of the Madison River, opening out to a broad, flat plain and the thermal valley around the Firehole River. As you move southward from Madison Junction, trails lead to thermal features in the Lower, Midway, and Upper Geyser Basins, as well as waterfalls, lakes, and meadows. Bison and elk spend the entire year along the Firehole River, wintering near the warmth of the geyser basins and summering in such places as Buffalo Meadows and Little Firehole Meadows. Shoshone Lake is the park's largest backcountry lake, home to an array of waterbirds, moose, elk, deer, otters, mink, weasels, and planted lake trout and brown trout. On the west shore is Shoshone Geyser Basin.

The Bechler and Falls River area of the park, reached through Ashton, Idaho, is also called Cascade Corner, boasting many of the park's waterfalls. Vegetation thrives in this low, wet region, attracting the likes of black bears, cranes, herons, moose, deer, and elk. The most enjoyable time to explore is from late August into fall, when the meadows have dried up, the streams gone down, and the mosquitoes thinned out.

In the Snake River and Heart Lake areas, the headwaters of the Snake River wind through pristine meadows, marshes, and one of the park's most dramatic displays of burned trees. You may see elk feeding on the high meadows of Big Game Ridge, wind-shaped pines atop Mount Sheridan, and Rustic Geyser erupting on the shore of Heart Lake. This is not an area for casual hikers; there are steep ridges, long distances, and lots of streams and rivers to cross. The best time to travel here is in August and September when the streams, rivers, and mosquitoes have subsided.

In the Thorofare area, you'll be south of the remote Southeast Arm of Yellowstone Lake, south of the wild marshes and meadows of the Upper Yellowstone River, and in sight of the snowy summits of Yellowstone's highest peaks. The lake is home to native cutthroat trout, which attract pelicans, otters, minks, mergansers, cormorants, gulls, ospreys, eagles, and even grizzly bears. You can be ferried to five remote campsites on the south shore of Lake Yellowstone from the Bridge Bay Marina for $106 each way. Contact the marina (307/242-3880, mid-May–Sept.) or the Central Backcountry Office (307/344-2160 or 307/344-2163) for more information. The upper Yellowstone River flows into the Southeast Arm. Its delta is home to sandhill cranes, great blue herons, Canada geese, and a variety of ducks. Moose, elk, bear, and wolves live throughout the valley. Artifacts left by native people include old tepee rings and lean-tos dating back 10,000 years. These should never be disturbed.

Will we have any problems with animals in the wilderness?

Since this is grizzly country, you'll need to take some precautions for your safety and the continued well-being of our bears. The first thing to do is minimize the bears' attraction to you and your food while you're in the backcountry. This means keeping a clean campsite. Suspend all food items and odorous items on supplied poles or 10 feet above ground and 4 feet out from tree trunks; don't sleep in the same clothes you wore while cooking; store all food in airtight containers; avoid smelly foods and items (tuna, bacon, ham, lotions, deodorants, and the like); and never eat or store food in your tent.

If you intend to travel and camp in the backcountry, you should read about bears (see the *For Further Reading* section of the *Quick Reference* chapter) so you know a little more about their habits. If you're worried about a bear encounter, inquire at a ranger station or visitor center for recommendations of trails less likely to have bear activity and for precautions to take while traveling in bear country.

Bear attacks are rare, and most are caused by three situations: surprising a bear, getting between a mother and her cubs, and getting too close to a bear that has food. The chances of being attacked are very small. But, if you do encounter a bear, follow this advice:

- Don't run or make sudden movements.
- Back away slowly; arm your bear spray.
- Talk quietly to the bear; don't shout.
- Don't drop your pack.
- Avoid looking directly at the bear.
- If the bear charges you, *freeze*. Drop to the ground, lift your legs to your chest, clasp your hands behind your neck, and lie still.
- As a last line of defense, aim and discharge bear spray.

If you're traveling in Yellowstone's backcountry, buy bear spray. It's been effective in over 90 percent of reported cases where it was used. You can buy a canister of the spray (300 grams) at any of the Yellowstone General Stores in the park or at any sporting goods store in the surrounding gateway communities. The spray is designed to stop an attacking bear. It should not be applied to people, tents, or packs as a repellent. Carry it on your belt or in your hand, not inside a pack.

Bear Management Areas have been established throughout the park for the purpose of reducing human impacts on some of our prime grizzly bear habitats. Allowing bears to pursue natural behavior and activities, free from human disturbance and interruption, is good for visitors and bears alike. Some restrictions in these areas might include: area and trail closures, a recommended party size of four or more people, and a prohibition of travel except during daylight hours and on established trails. For more information and a locator map, see the *Bear Management Areas in Yellowstone* section of the *Quick Reference* chapter.

In recent years, bison have injured more people than bears have. Take my advice, and always give them room. Moose, elk, and even deer can be protective of their young and their space. Feeding coyotes and wolves can make them dangerous. They should be treated with the respect due any large carnivore.

VI.
Recreational Opportunities

What's there to do around here?

The size of Yellowstone can be overwhelming. Almost everything in the park is on a grand scale—mountains, lakes, forests, herds of bison and elk, grizzly bears. Although you can't take a helicopter ride to get a bird's-eye view, you can choose activities at different times of the year that allow you to see and enjoy the park on your own terms.

Driving

A leisurely drive through Yellowstone, with stops at major features, can serve as an introduction to the big picture.

Bicycling

More than 300 miles of steep, winding, narrow roadways are available to bicyclists starting from the third Friday in April, weather conditions permitting, to October. Or, for the most avid cyclists, the road between the West Entrance and Mammoth Hot Springs (only) is open to non-motorized travel from about mid-March until the third Thursday in April. You can pedal your way through the park's varied terrain, and huff and puff along elevations that range 5,300–8,860 feet. Besides the developed roadways, there are 12 designated bike trails inside the park and three gravel roads that are great for mountain biking. No bikes are allowed on backcountry trails or on boardwalks.

Walking and Hiking

A journey on our 1,200 miles of walking trails begins with a single step. From strolls through meadows of summer wildflowers

to steep hikes up snowy summits, these many paths take you through Yellowstone's most spectacular landscapes and backcountry areas. For those who want to stay close to the main features in the park, there are plenty of short walks and boardwalks.

Boating, Floating, Paddling, and Boat Tours

In the summer, boating or float tubing can be fun ways to explore some of the park's lakes—just remember that all the streams and rivers, except the channel between Lewis and Shoshone Lakes, are off-limits to boating. Make sure you're prepared for some of the cold-est water tempera-

tures and swiftest currents anywhere. You can rent rowboats and motorboats and take scenic-cruiser tours of Yellowstone Lake out of Bridge Bay Marina; bring your own float or boat; or paddle quietly on the big lakes in a kayak or canoe with a licensed outfitter.

Fishing

You don't have to go far in Yellowstone to cast a line into some of the best fish-ing waters in North America, whether pond, lake, or stream. The park has over 400 fishable spots, offering about 800 miles of flowing trout waters, including the Yellowstone, Firehole, and Madison Rivers, and 45 fishable lakes, such as Shoshone, Lewis, Heart, and Yellowstone. If you want to escape the crowds, simply take a short hike from the road, and you'll be alone on some of the most scenic waterways. Permits

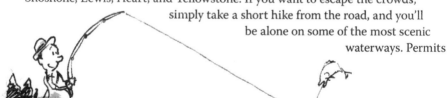

are sold at Yellowstone General Stores. Fishing comes in many forms in the park, from guided day fish-ing trips on Yellowstone Lake to multiple-day fishing trips into the backcountry led by licensed outfitters to an hour at your own secluded paradise.

Swimming

Although swimming seems like a natural activity in a place with so much

water, it can be risky. Our rivers, streams, and lakes are so cold that hypothermia is a real danger to swimmers. We generally discourage visitors from taking the plunge. Waters that are strictly off-limits include any of the park's thermal features and any streams whose waters flow from thermal features. Since we don't have swimming pools, my best advice to swimmers is to find another diversion while you're here.

Horseback Riding

A horseback ride around Yellowstone is bound to be an unforgettable trip. We have lots of opportunities to horse-pack in the park, on your own or with an outfitter who's licensed to guide wilderness trips. For milder excursions, take a one-to two-hour horse trail ride with a wrangler/guide from one of the corrals, located at Mammoth Hot Springs, Canyon Village, and Roosevelt Lodge.

Winter Sports

One of the park's best-kept secrets is its range of winter activities. You can cross-country ski on all unplowed roads from Mammoth Hot Springs or the Old Faithful Snow Lodge, visiting the park's five warming huts along the way. You can take guided ski tours, snowshoe tours, or snowmobile rides to some spectacular areas. You can glide around the ice rink at Mammoth Hot Springs. Or you can have a winter adventure with the Yellowstone Association Institute, which leads tours exploring the park's unique winter ecology.

How much of the park is accessible to hikers?

Most of the park is accessible to hikers, but, unless you have the survival instincts of a bear, you have to be an expert with map and compass to travel off the trails. When you hike the Yellowstone trails, you're carrying on a tradition that goes back thousands of years—Indians, early visitors, and generations of backpackers and hikers have trekked here. Our trails are your best shot at an insider's look at Yellowstone.

Most of the park's 2.2 million acres are wild, rugged backcountry with plenty of waterfalls, wildlife, inspiring scenery, and thermal basins for the curious hiker. To enjoy your experience, you'll need to take responsibility for your own safety and for preserving this dynamic and fragile national park.

Here are a few hints for getting the most out of your hiking adventure:

- Begin your hike by stopping at a ranger station or visitor center for information on current trail conditions and bear activity. Trails can be temporarily closed due to unexpected weather, bear activity, or fire. It's best to be an informed hiker, not a disappointed one.

- Take safety in numbers when you hike in bear country. It's best to hike with friends, make noise, and stay alert to help protect yourselves and the well-being of our wild animals. (See *Bear Management Areas in Yellowstone* in the *Quick Reference* chapter.)

- Plan your hike so you don't travel long distances without allowing adequate time to rest and enjoy the spectacular scenery. Don't be surprised if your progress slows because of fallen trees across the trails.

- Pay special attention in burned areas, where sudden gusts of wind may topple standing dead trees, and in thermal areas, where thin crusts of ground can break, dropping away to scalding water.

- Help keep our backcountry areas clean for everyone by packing out all your trash.

- Carry enough drinking water for your hike. Untreated stream and lake water may not be safe to drink.

Now, let's go hiking!

What do we need to know about hiking in Yellowstone?

You can escape the crowds by hiking away from Yellowstone's main roads and visitor areas into one of world's most awesome wilderness areas. But be aware of some precautions, so that your hike is an enjoyable and safe experience.

Our clear, cold streams can be deceiving. Even though the water looks good enough to drink, it may harbor organisms that will make you regret the first gulp. *Giardia* and *Campylobacter* bacteria can cause mild to really debilitating intestinal distress. So, if you can't boil fresh water for 3–5 minutes, treat it with iodine or filter it (maximum effective filter pore size for *Giardia* is five microns); otherwise, carry ample treated water.

Crossing fast-moving rivers and streams poses a second challenge for hikers. To keep our wilderness wild, most trails that cross park waterways are not bridged. As a result, you might need to wade to the other side. Many hikers bring along old running shoes or river sandals, because wet hiking boots can turn into frozen boots by the next morning. Whatever you do, don't try a barefoot crossing. It can be painful and make it difficult to keep your balance. If you can't roll your pants up enough to keep them dry, take them off or wear shorts. You don't necessarily have to cross where the trail meets the water; you'll often find an easier crossing upstream or down. If a ford is more than thigh deep, forget it. It's just not worth the danger you'd put yourself in. Always check with the nearest ranger station or visitor center for current trail conditions.

Yellowstone's summer weather is, at best, extremely volatile. One minute it's hot and sunny, the next it's raining, and then, suddenly, you can find yourself pelted by hail, wind, and snow. A well-prepared hiker is ready for the most extreme changes in weather. For more detailed information on hiking in the park, pick up a copy of *Yellowstone Trails* by Mark C. Marschall.

What should we take on our hike?

H ere's a rundown on day-hiking essentials in summer:

Clothing
Start with a pair of sturdy, comfortable sneakers with good traction or light-weight boots or hiking shoes. Shorts are popular for hiking, but if the weather changes you'll be glad to have a pair of loose pants made of material that dries quickly, such as nylon, nylon/cotton blend, or light wool. A long-sleeved polyester shirt and a polyester/fleece vest or a wool sweater are good for layering. A waterproof and wind-proof shell with attached hood is essential in case the weather turns windy, cold, or wet. Inside your pack include a rainsuit and a warm hat to keep your head dry and prevent heat loss if the weather changes.

Equipment
A small daypack, knapsack, or fanny pack and plenty of water are essential, especially in hot weather and on difficult hikes. Non-odorous snacks are a good idea, particularly when hungry children are along for the hike. Whatever you bring, remember to pack out all your trash. Other essentials are insect repellent, sunscreen, lip balm, sunglasses, and a first-aid kit or just a few bandages to take care of any scrapes and cuts. Sometimes a hike lasts longer than you expect; instead of having to find your way back in the dark, pack a headlamp.

Once you're away from the visitor areas, your only bathroom amenity is the toilet paper you carry with you. Human waste must be buried at least six inches deep, 100 feet or more from any water and trail. A light trowel helps.

Depending upon your interests, you can bring along other items that will make your adventures more interesting, such as field books, binoculars, a camera, and fishing gear. If you plan to go off-trail, a map, compass, fire starter, signal mirror, knife, and police whistle—and the know-how to use them—are vital tools. Trekking poles can add stability.

Day hikes are one thing; backpacking trips are a whole other species. A jaunt into the backcountry for several days will require some careful planning of equipment and clothes. For backcountry essentials, see the *Camping and Backpacking* chapter and the *Backcountry Regulations* and *Bear Management Areas in Yellowstone* sections of the *Quick Reference* chapter. You can also get a free Backcountry Trip Planner through the Central Backcountry Office (P.O. Box 168, Yellowstone National Park, WY, 82190, 307/344-2160 or 307/344-2163, www.nps.gov/yell/planyourvisit/backcountryhiking.htm).

If you're looking for an easy trail that takes no more than 2.5–3 hours, the following chart will give you some suggestions. These popular hikes follow easy trails that won't wipe you out for the rest of the day. The trailheads are easy to find, with spectacular views or scenic photo spots, some picnic areas, and plenty of ways to hop onto other good trails. All of them are good for families with children, and some have the bonus of waterfalls or a place to fish. For trails in our geyser basins, see the *What's the best way to see the geysers?* section of the *Park Attractions* chapter.

HIKE (BY AREA)	DISTANCE (ROUND-TRIP)	DIFFICULTY	STARTS FROM
Bechler Area			
Bechler Falls	2 miles	easy	end of Cave Falls Road
Canyon Area			
Crystal Falls	0.25 mile	easy	North Rim Trail
Lower Falls	1 mile	easy	Uncle Tom's parking area
Fishing Bridge Area			
Pelican Creek	1 mile	easy	Pelican Creek Bridge
Storm Point	2 miles	easy	Indian Pond turnout
Howard Eaton Trail	7 miles	easy	Fishing Bridge Visitor Center
Lamar (Northeast Area)			
Trout Lake Campground	1 mile	moderately easy	1.3 miles south of Pebble Creek
Mammoth Hot Springs Area			
Wraith Falls Area	1 mile	easy	east of Lava Creek Picnic
Norris Area			
Artist Paint Pots Meadows	1 mile	moderately easy	4.5 miles south of Norris on Norris-Madison Rd.
Old Faithful Area			
Fairy Falls	5 miles	easy	Steel Bridge Parking
Lone Star Geyser	5 miles	easy	Kepler Cascades
Mystic Falls	2.4 miles	moderately easy	Biscuit Basin Loop Trail
Tower-Roosevelt Area			
Lost Creek Falls	0.5 mile	easy	Roosevelt Lodge
Tower Falls Trail	1 mile	moderately easy	Tower Falls General Store parking area
Yellowstone River Picnic Area Trail	4 miles	easy-moderate	Yellowstone River Picnic Area

These trails are a bit tougher than the easy hikes, requiring more time or a little more oomph to walk up moderate slopes and occasional steep parts. Families with children are welcome to have a go; just make sure you have plenty of water and snacks. Many of these treks will lead you to awesome scenery, waterfalls, great wildlife viewing, and lakes to fish in during the summer months.

HIKE (BY AREA)	DISTANCE	DIFFICULTY (ROUND-TRIP)	STARTS FROM
Canyon Area			
Cascade Lake Trail	4.4 miles	moderate	Cascade Lake Trail Picnic
Grebe Lake	6 miles	moderate	Norris-Canyon Road
Grant Village Area			
Riddle Lake	5 miles	moderate	south of Grant Village
Lamar (Northeast Area)			
Pebble Creek Trail	4 miles	moderate	Pebble Creek Bridge
Slough Creek	4 miles	moderate	Slough Creek Campground, off Northeast Entrance Rd.
Mammoth Hot Springs Area			
Beaver Ponds Loop	5 miles	moderate	Clematis Gulch near Liberty Cap
Hidden Falls	5 miles	moderate	Mammoth-Tower Road
Lava Creek	7 miles	moderate	Lava Creek Picnic Area
Osprey Falls	8 miles	moderate	Old Bunsen Peak Road Trail
Madison Junction Area			
Fairy Falls	5 miles	moderate	Fountain Flats Road
Norris Area			
Grizzly Lake Trail	4 miles	moderate	1 mile south of Beaver Lake on Norris-Mammoth Rd.
Old Faithful Area			
Delacy Creek/Shoshone Lake	6 miles	moderate	DeLacy Creek
Snake River Area			
Shoshone Lake	4.5 miles	moderate	north of Lewis Lake
Tower-Roosevelt Area			
Hellroaring Creek	4 miles	moderately strenuous	Hellroaring Parking Area/ west of Tower Junction
Lost Lake Loop	4 miles	moderately strenuous	Roosevelt Lodge
Mount Washburn	6 miles	moderately strenuous	Dunraven Pass

What are some great butt-kicking hikes?

If you like to get your heart really pumping and feel the burn in your legs, here's a list of some wilderness trails that will happily oblige. You'll need to be in good shape and carefully plan your trip for these babies, but they'll pay you back with some spectacular scenery and a feeling of accomplishment once you're finished. Most of these trips can be done in a day, but many also have overnight camping areas along the way. Just be sure you have the time and energy before embarking on these journeys, as most of them have strenuous uphill climbs, some river crossings, and higher elevations, which mean much more huffing and puffing.

TRAIL

HIKE (BY AREA)	DISTANCE	DIFFICULTY (ROUND-TRIP)	STARTS FROM
Bechler River Area			
Ouzel Falls	14 miles	strenuous	Bechler River Ranger Station
Union and Morning Falls	16 miles	strenuous	Grassy Lake Reservoir, near Flagg Ranch
Dunanda/Silver Scarf Falls	18 miles	strenuous	Bechler River Ranger Station
Canyon Area			
Red Rock Trail	1.5 miles	strenuous	Lookout Point Overlook
Observation Peak	11 miles	strenuous	Cascade Lake Picnic Area
Seven-Mile Hole Trail	11 miles	strenuous	Glacial Boulder, Inspiration Point Rd.
East Entrance			
Avalanche Peak Trail	5 miles	strenuous	Eleanor Lake, on East Entrance Rd.
Fishing Bridge Area			
Elephant Back Mountain Trail	3 miles	moderately strenuous	1 mile south of Fishing Bridge Junction
Pelican Valley Trail	16 miles	moderately strenuous	Pelican Valley Trailhead
Madison Junction			
Purple Mountain Trail	6 miles	strenuous	0.25 mi north of Madison Junction on Madison-Norris Rd.
Mammoth Hot Springs Area			
Bunsen Peak	10 miles	strenuous	Old Bunsen Peak Road, 5 miles south of Mammoth
Sepulcher Mountain	11 miles	strenuous	Clematis Gulch near Liberty Cap
Norris Area			
Solfatara Creek Trail	13 miles	strenuous	Norris Campground
Old Faithful Area			
Shoshone Lake Loop	17.5 miles	moderately strenuous	Lone Star Trailhead

Can we mountain bike in Yellowstone?

The good news for mountain bikers is that you can ride more than 300 miles of roadway in the park, including the main public roads, three gravel roads, and 12 bike trails located throughout the park. The bad news is that only a few are well suited for mountain biking: the gravel roads, the Old Gardiner Road, Blacktail Plateau Drive, and Bunsen Peak Road. Without express permission, all park trails, off-road backcountry areas, service roads, and utility corridors are off limits to bicycles. Your window of opportunity for biking lasts from the third Friday in April, weather conditions permitting, through October, barring early snowstorms. Or, for intrepid mountain bikers, the road between the West Entrance and Mammoth Hot Springs (only) is open to non-motorized travel from about mid-March until the third Thursday in April. In a typical weather year, the best times to ride in Yellowstone are the clear, cool days of September and October, when traffic is lighter.

Bicycle touring is becoming popular, because the park offers long country rides and challenging climbs in road elevations that range 5,300–8,860 feet. The most notable are Craig Pass (8,261 feet), Sylvan Pass (8,530 feet), and Dunraven Pass (8,859 feet).

The park's narrow, rough, shoulderless roads can be challenging for novice bikers. Add some high snow banks in May and June, especially in the south-central area of the park, and cycling can be downright dangerous. Other hazards include heavy summer traffic, which usually results in at least a few bike-versus-car accidents each year. It's best to avoid peak traffic periods

(mid-morning–late afternoon) on the roads that serve the main points of interest in the park. Riding at the crack of dawn can be awesome.

For specific information on the routes, or to download the Bicycling in Yellowstone National Park brochure, visit the National Park Service website page devoted to bicycling (www.nps.gov/yell/planyourvisit/bicycling.htm). For information on current weather or road conditions, services, and facilities, call Park Information anytime (307/344-7381), or stop by any ranger station or visitor center during business hours.

Guided mountain bike tours led by knowledgeable guides are offered by a variety of companies and cater to all levels of ability. Most tours provide a mountain bike, helmet, water bottle, and instruction in biking techniques and trail etiquette. Some companies have family outings and may provide child trailers. For a list of licensed bicycle outfitting companies, refer to the *Licensed Tour Operators and Outfitters* section of the *Quick Reference* chapter, or consult the National Park Service website (www.nps.gov/yell/planyourvisit/bikebusn.htm).

Repair services and bicycle rentals are available in the gateway communities of West Yellowstone, Bozeman, and Livingston, Montana, and Jackson and Cody, Wyoming. Rental prices range $15–25 for a full day, $12–16 for a half day, or $3.50–4 per hour. Most shops include a helmet, tool kit, and water bottle, but it's best to ask.

Before you ride off into the distance, here are a few rules and safety precautions:

- Bicycle riders on public roadways in Yellowstone National Park must obey the same rules and regulations as motor vehicle drivers.
- Bicycles are not allowed on any park trails or off-road in backcountry areas. Service roads and utility corridors are closed to bikes unless use is expressly permitted.
- Bicycles must exhibit a white light in front and a red light or reflector on the rear during periods of low visibility.
- Riding abreast on a public roadway is prohibited. Ride single file.
- Riders should wear a helmet and high-visibility clothing.
- Bicyclists must pull over and allow motorists to pass if the cyclists are impeding traffic flow.
- Bicyclists must yield the right-of-way to hikers and horse riders.
- The maximum number of cyclists traveling in a single cluster may not exceed 15, and clusters must be at least half a mile apart.

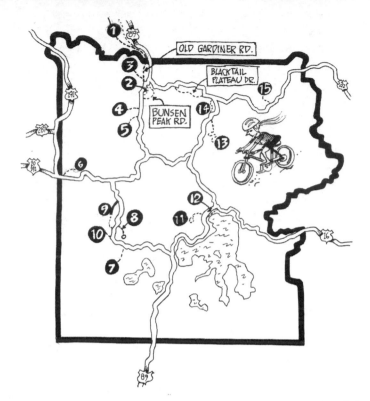

1. Disused railroad bed along Yellowstone River, Gardiner–Reese Creek (park boundary). 5 mi.

2. Service road, Golden Gate–Joffee Lake. 1.5 mi.

3. Mammoth service road, Old Gardiner Road–microwave station. 1.5 mi.

4. Swan Lake gravel pit road, 6 mi. south of Mammoth. 1 mi.

5. Superintendent's campground road (adjacent to Indian Creek Campground). 0.4 mi.

6. Riverside trail, West Entrance–Barns Road. 1.4 mi.

7. Lone Star Geyser parking lot. 2 mi.

8. Paved trail, Lower Yellowstone General Store at Old Faithful–Morning Glory Pool. 2 mi. Bicycles prohibited on unpaved trail continuing beyond Morning Glory Pool.

9. Fountain Freight Road, 6 mi. north of Old Faithful. 5 mi.

10. Disused service road, Daisy Geyser–Biscuit Basin. 1 mi.

11. Natural Bridge Road near Bridge Bay. 1 mi.

12. Old lakeshore roadbed, Lake Hotel–main road south of Lake Junction. 1 mi.

13. Mt. Washburn Service Road, Chittenden Road parking area–Mt. Washburn summit. 3 mi. Bicycles prohibited on trail between summit and Dunraven Pass parking area.

14. Old Chittenden Service Road, Grand Loop Road–Tower Falls Campground. 2 mi.

15. Rose Creek Service Road behind Lamar Ranger Station. 1 mi.

Can we go boating in Yellowstone?

If your idea of a perfect vacation is rowing, paddling, sailing, or motoring the waters of Yellowstone, then you're in luck. You can do all of the above, although not everywhere. All park rivers and streams are closed to boating except the Lewis River channel between Lewis Lake and Shoshone Lake, and motor-driven boats are permitted only on Lewis Lake and Yellowstone Lake (the South, Southeast, and Flat Mountain Arms are off limits). Non-motorized boats are allowed in all other lakes in the park, but Shoshone Lake is the only backcountry lake that's accessible to a roadside boat launch area (at Lewis Lake). Sorry, no jet skis, water-skiing, airboats, or the like are allowed in Yellowstone National Park.

A permit is required for all vessels (motorized and non-motorized including float tubes) and must be obtained in person at any of the following locations: South Entrance, Lewis Lake Campground, Grant Village Backcountry Office, and Bridge Bay Ranger Station. Non-motorized boating permits are available at West Entrance, Northeast Entrance, Mammoth Backcountry Office, Old Faithful Backcountry Office, Canyon Backcountry Office, Bechler Ranger Station, West Contact Station, West Yellowstone Chamber of Commerce, and locations where motorized permits are sold. The fee is $20 (annual) or $10 (seven-day) for motorized vessels and $10 (annual) or $5 (seven-day) for non-motorized vessels.

A few rules to follow: Private vessels may be no longer than 40 feet, you may not anchor or beach boats overnight without a backcountry permit, and you may not operate your vessel more than 45 miles per hour. For a brochure on boating regulations in Yellowstone, visit the NPS website (www.nps.gov/yell/planyourvisit/boating.htm)

You can launch motorized and hand-powered boats on Yellowstone Lake at Bridge Bay Marina, along the north shore, and at Grant Village on the west shore; on Lewis Lake, launch them on the southeast shore. Hand-carried boats may be launched and removed at Sedge Bay on the northeast shore of

Yellowstone Lake. The channel between Lewis and Shoshone Lakes can be paddled most of the way, but the final mile requires a towline or portage, and that stretch can get even longer during summer and fall, when water levels are low. Sailboats launched at Bridge Bay Marina have to retract their masts to get under the bridge into Yellowstone Lake. Call the Bridge Bay Backcountry Office (307/242-2413) or the Central Backcountry Office (307/344-2160 or 307/344-2163) for more information.

Through Xanterra Parks & Resorts you can rent rowboats and outboards and hire guides at the Bridge Bay Marina mid-June–September, or you can take a one-hour scenic-cruiser tour of Lake Yellowstone that departs day or evening early June– September. Scenic-cruiser tour prices are $11.25 for adults, $7 for kids 2–11 years old, and kids under two ride free. A 16-foot rowboat (holding up to four people) rents for $43 for an eight-hour day or $9.50 per hour; an 18-foot outboard with a 40-horsepower engine (2–6 people) rents for $45 per hour. You can take a guided fishing trip in a 22-foot cabin cruiser (up to six people) for $140 for two hours up to $840 for 12 hours, or in a 34-foot cabin cruiser (up to six people) for $180 for two hours up to $1,080 for 12 hours. You can also rent dock space at the Bridge Bay Marina (307/242-3880, 8 A.M.–8 P.M.) late May–September for $9 per night for boats 16 feet and under and $12 per night for boats more than 16 feet. Many companies offer guided wilderness trips on Yellowstone's waterways; check the *Licensed Tour Operators and Outfitters* section of the *Quick Reference* chapter, or consult the Park Service website (www.nps.gov/yell/planyourvisit/boatbusn.htm).

Caution is the best policy when you take to our waters, since more than a hundred people have lost their lives in the park's frigid lakes. With summer water temperatures ranging 40–60°F, hypothermia is always a threat. Add sudden, powerful winds and storms that whip waves five or six feet high, and you'll see that boating here is not for the faint of heart.

Here are a few suggestions to keep your Yellowstone boating experience as safe as possible

- In hand-propelled craft, travel close to shore and within sight and hearing of other party members.
- Begin early in the morning, and make open-water crossings before afternoon winds come up.
- Wait out rough water; storms often subside in the late afternoon and evening.
- Keep loads to a minimum; overloaded boats are dangerous and against regulations. Distribute your load evenly, and keep your load low.
- Always carry a bailing device and an extra paddle.
- Get off the water during strong winds and lightning storms.
- Travel in a group and stay within voice-carrying distance.
- Place at least one experienced boater in each boat.
- Be sure to have a well-maintained, easily accessible, U.S. Coast Guard–approved flotation device for each person on board. If you're canoeing, wear one.

What do we need to know about fishing in the park?

You need to know that you're in for some of the finest, most scenic trout fishing in the world. Take your pick from the park's 400 fishable waters, and, whether you're a novice or master angler, spin or fly fisher, you're likely to find an enthusiastic trout at the other end of your line.

Our fishing habitats comprise about 800 miles of flowing rivers and streams, such as the famous Yellowstone, Firehole, and Madison Rivers. Many of the park's hundreds of lakes were stocked with trout from the 1890s to the 1950s, but some could not sustain a healthy fish population through the bitter winters. Today there are 120 fishable lakes, including Shoshone, the largest backcountry lake in the lower 48 states, and Yellowstone, where the cutthroat trout average over 15 inches.

Within the park, you'll find wild native cutthroat, whitefish, rare sail-finned grayling, as well as exotic rainbow, brown, brook, and lake trout. The average size of fish landed in Yellowstone is currently around 14 inches. Some waters are designated "catch-and-release" and others "fly-fishing only." More than half of the park's landed fish are caught in Yellowstone Lake and Yellowstone River.

Our fishing season opens on the Saturday of Memorial Day weekend, and ends the first Sunday of November. Exceptions are Yellowstone Lake, which opens June 1, and its tributary streams and the Yellowstone River (above the falls), which open July 15.

Anyone 16 years or older is required to have a Yellowstone National Park Fishing Permit ($15 for a three-day permit, $20 for a seven-day permit, or $35 for a season permit). Anglers 12–15 years of age need a non-fee permit. You can pick up permits at ranger stations, visitor centers, and Yellowstone Park General Stores. State fishing licenses are not required in the park, and they cannot be used in lieu of Yellowstone permits.

The park's fishing regulations are meant both to ensure a happy and fruitful fishing trip for you and to nurture Yellowstone's ecosystem by preserving and restoring natural habitats, populations, and distributions. After all, the park houses a few native anglers, such as bald eagles, ospreys, otters, pelicans, and grizzly bears, whose survival hinges on a healthy fish population. Fortunately, human anglers are now doing their part by releasing more than 90 percent of the fish they catch in park waters. You need to be aware of a few current issues: We're changing fishing regulations to prevent cutthroat from being displaced by lake trout in Yellowstone Lake; we've implemented a nontoxic policy that bans the use of split-shot sinkers, weighted jigs, and soft lead–weighted ribbon; and we're working to combat invasive Aquatic Nuisance Species, such as the whirling disease parasite, by educating anglers about known invaders and their locations, as well as the need to clean all gear after fishing. For more information on fishing regulations, contact the Chief Ranger's Office (P.O. Box 168, Yellowstone National Park, WY 82190, 307/344-2105) or visit the NPS website (www.nps.gov/yell/planyourvisit/fishing.htm).

For a list of fishing outfitters who can give you a worry free angling experience in Yellowstone, refer to the *Licensed Tour Operators and Outfitters* section of the *Quick Reference* chapter, or consult the NPS website (www.nps.gov/yell/planyourvisit/fishbsn.htm).

Welcome to paradise. Before starting out on a fishing expedition, check at a ranger station or visitor center for current fishing regulations and a license, and at the tackle shops in the gateway communities for equipment, advice, and information. Recommended reading is the *Yellowstone Fishing Guide* by Robert Charlton. He divides the park into six zones that correspond to the major watersheds.

The Gallatin and Gardiner watersheds (Zone 1) have the only places where kids can try their luck with worm bait—in the Gardiner River and in Obsidian, Indian, and Panther Creeks. For a popular and easily accessible pond with brook and cutthroat trout near Mammoth, try Blacktail Ponds, where the native cutthroats are protected by a catch-and-release policy. Cottonwood Creek, a 12-mile hike up the Yellowstone River Trail near the park's north boundary, offers excellent fishing for cutthroat averaging 13 inches. The Gardiner River has small brook trout above Osprey Falls and bigger prizes in the pocket water below the falls.

The Lamar River and Soda Butte Creek watersheds (Zone 2) are best fished after the early summer snowmelt. Slough Creek and Soda Butte Creek are both great trout fishing streams and are easily accessed from the Northeast Entrance Road. Some of the best cutthroat angling is near Slough Creek Campground, where the fish average 12–13 inches. And who could resist a lake named Trout, located near the Pebble Creek Campground off the Northeast Entrance Road. You can walk in on an easy, 0.5-mile trail.

The Gibbon and Firehole River watersheds (Zone 3) are where these two rivers join in National Park Meadow to create the Madison River, which flows for 14 miles inside the park. The Firehole River is warmed by geothermal waters, and some of our bison and elk spend the entire year there. The Gibbon River heads at Grebe Lake, where you might catch and release a grayling after an easy three-mile hike in. You can also try your luck for rainbow and grayling at nearby Wolf Lake, provided you keep an eye out for grizzlies. Each of these rivers is easily accessed from park roads; the West Entrance Road follows the Madison east to Madison Junction, then tracks the Gibbon north to Norris Geyser Basin. Grand Loop Road follows the Firehole River south from Madison Junction to Old Faithful.

The Firehole is one of the most popular fly-fishing streams in the park, with healthy populations of rainbow, brown, and brook trout as well as whitefish. Favorite holes and runs include Muleshoe Bend, Firehole Canyon, and around Fountain Flats Freight Road. Upstream from Goose and Feather Lakes, you'll find some deep runs and riffles, and there's good dry fly-fishing from the Midway Geyser Basin up to Morning Glory Pool. Note that July and August aren't the best months to fish the river, because the water warms up and the fish retreat.

For smaller fish, the Gibbon offers some good spots, including the one-mile Virginia Meadows stretch above Virginia Cascades, which is a popular place to picnic and give kids a chance to fly-fish for pan-size brook trout. For larger fish, try the Elk Park and Gibbon Meadow sections, south of Norris.

The Madison, restricted to fly-fishing inside the park, is one of the West's most famous rivers. Here you'll find brown, rainbow, cutthroat, and brook trout, with spring and fall runs of rainbows, browns, and whitefish. Great fishing spots include the holes around National Park Meadows and some unofficially named ones: Nine-Mile Hole, Seven-Mile Run, Cable Car Run, and the "Barns Holes." The most popular time to fish the Madison is during the fall spawning run up from Hebgen Lake, five miles north of West Yellowstone.

The Yellowstone River watershed from Inspiration Point to a place one-mile downstream from the Yellowstone Lake outlet (Zone 4) is home to some of the best cutthroat fishing. The river here is closed to fishing until July 15 to protect spawning trout. Easy access is along Grand Loop Road, which closely follows the river from Lake Yellowstone to Canyon. A popular spot for excellent catch-and-release cutthroat and grayling fishing is Cascade Lake in the Canyon area. At the east end of the lake there's a gathering place for spawning grayling in early June. The most scenic access is along the 2.5-mile Cascade Creek Trail, home to a popular 8.7-mile stretch of the Yellowstone River for catch-and-release fishing. Be prepared to compete with other anglers, and get to know the regulations because some areas are closed to fishing to protect wildlife. You can get to the west bank from Grand Loop Road between Canyon and Fishing Bridge; to reach the east bank, you can follow the Howard Eaton Trail from Fishing Bridge or Canyon. The Buffalo Ford Picnic Area provides easy-access angling, and the most popular area is between Fishing Bridge and Sulphur Cauldron, where cutthroats average over 15 inches. This area accounts for 80 percent of the river's total fishing activity.

Park waters on the west slope of the Continental Divide (Zone 5) include three major lakes (Lewis, Shoshone, and Heart) and four rivers (Lewis, Bechler, Falls, and the Snake). Shoshone Lake is the largest backcountry lake in the lower 48 states and the most popular backcountry destination in the park. The Bechler, Falls, and Snake Rivers are all hike-in fisheries, with plentiful waterfalls around the Bechler and Falls. Access is via Ashton, Idaho, from Cave Falls Road and Reclamation Road for the Bechler and Falls Rivers and via the South Entrance Road for the Snake River and Lewis Lake.

Two backcountry cutthroat lakes, Beula and Hering, are accessible from the Huckleberry Springs turnoff near Flagg Ranch. Falls Creek is popular with local fly fishers, and Falls River has some awesome cutthroat and rainbow fishing, but it requires a bit of a hike. For easy-access lake fishing, try Lewis Lake for lake trout and browns. An eight-mile hike from the South Entrance Road takes you past some interesting geothermal areas to Heart Lake, where you'll find cutthroat, lake trout, and whitefish. The Lewis-Shoshone Channel can provide trophy fishing in the fall, with brown trout averaging 16 inches. Try the scenic area between Lewis Lake and Lewis Falls for good pool and riffle fishing for smaller trout. Mountain Ash Creek in the Bechler area is an excellent spot to catch cutthroats and rainbows averaging over eight inches, while the south shore of Shoshone Lake is a great place for brown, lake, and brook trout averaging 17 inches. The late fall is a great time for large browns, but watch out for stormy weather.

The portion of the Yellowstone River watershed that includes Yellowstone Lake, from the park's southern boundary to a point one-mile downstream from the lake outlet (Zone 6), is home to the largest inland cutthroat population in the world. The lake's waters (7,733 elevation) are chilling year-round, yet they provide 50 percent of the entire park's fishing activity. Lake trout, evidently planted surreptitiously, threaten the Yellowstone Lake cutthroat population and all the fish-eaters (grizzly bears, ospreys, and others) that depend on them. Access by car is from the West Thumb-Fishing Bridge Road or the East Entrance Road. Boat access is from Bridge Bay Marina or the Grant Village boat ramp; foot and horse trail access is from the Thorofare Trail along the lake's east shore and the Trail Creek Trail, which you reach from the Heart Lake Trail off the east side of the South Entrance Road (25 miles each way).

There are numerous cutthroat-spawning tributary creeks around the lake, including Beaverdam, Cabin, Clear, Columbine, Cub, Grouse, Mountain, Raven, Trail, and Trappers. Some of the best cutthroat fishing is at Pelican Creek and Thorofare Creek, but the latter requires several days of hiking. Try your luck at Riddle and Sylvan Lakes, for catch-and-release angling only, or at Trail Lake near the southern tip of Yellowstone Lake's Southeast Arm, for wilderness fishing (two or three days' travel each way).

The average size of the lake's cutthroat population is 15 inches, with some over 20 inches. You can cast from both boat and shore, with the advantage going to the boaters. A favorite shore fishing area is along Gull Point Drive, south of Bridge Bay Campground, where a sandbar and shallow area provide a natural habitat for cutthroat. Yellowstone Lake gets 30–40 percent of the park's angler use, with the northwest portion of the lake the most heavily fished and the central and southern portions the least frequented. The more remote the area, the better your chances of catching bigger fish.

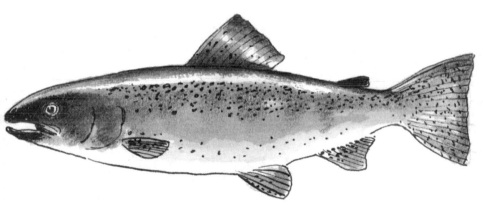

· Rainbow Trout ·

ZONE FISHING MAP

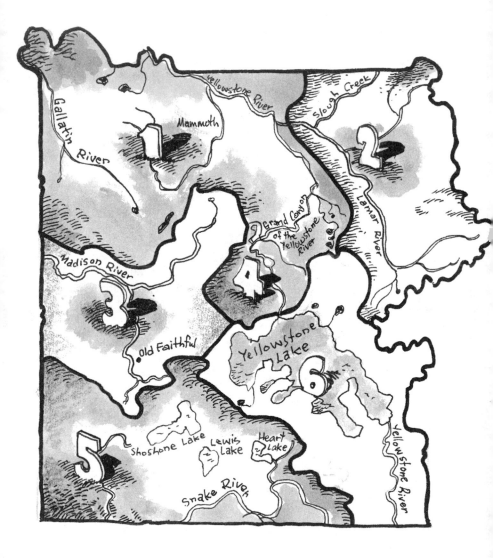

High in the saddle, you can get a unique perspective of Yellowstone without ever breaking a sweat. You'll also be part of a long park tradition because virtually all of the early exploration of Yellowstone was done on horseback.

Join one- or two-hour horseback trail rides offered at corrals located at Canyon (late June–August), Roosevelt Lodge (mid-June–August), and Mammoth Hot Springs (late May–mid-September). These unforgettable rides take you through some of the park's most beautiful areas, and you can even join an evening ride out of Mammoth and Canyon. The cost is $35 for a one-hour ride, $54 for a two-hour ride.

Roosevelt Lodge also offers one- or two-hour trail rides and horse-drawn wagon rides ending with its famous Old West Cookout, mid-June–August. The prices for one-hour horse rides are $66 for adults and $33 for children ages 8–11, for two hours you'll pay $80 for adults and $56 for children. Wagon rides cost $30 for adults and $18 for children ages 5–11 (children under five held on a lap are free). Contact Xanterra Parks & Resorts (307/344-7311 or 866/439-7375, www.travelyellowstone.com) for required reservations and information.

You can bring your own horse to Yellowstone. Most of the designated backcountry trails and about a hundred backcountry campsites are open to stock after July 1. However, stock animals are not allowed in any of the designated campgrounds in the park. Regulations are pretty tight on animals brought into the park, so be sure to learn the rules before hitting the trail (see the *Backcountry Regulations* section of the *Quick Reference* chapter). Call the Central Backcountry Office (307/344-2160 or 307/344-2163) for more information, or consult the horseback riding section of the NPS website (www.nps.gov/yell/planyourvisit/horseride.htm). From the site, you can download a useful brochure entitled "Horsepacking Information."

If you want a horseback experience but need a horse and guide, choose one of the many companies with years of experience taking horse pack trips into the Yellowstone wilderness. See the listings in the *Licensed Tour Operators and Outfitters* section of the *Quick Reference* chapter, or review the listings on the NPS website (www.nps.gov/yell/planyourvisit/stockbusn.htm).

Where can we ski in the park?

Cross-country skiers, start your engines; you can explore about 1,200 miles of backcountry trails and nearly 300 miles of roadways (shared with snowmobilers) during our winter months. The only road you can't ski during the winter is the one plowed road in the park, the North Entrance Road from Gardiner to Cooke City, Montana, at the northeast entrance of the park.

Our trails oblige all levels of skiers, and you can easily choose the route that best fits your skiing abilities by using our ski trail maps. They are available at the Old Faithful (307/545-2750) or Albright (307/344-2263) Visitor Center, the Central Backcountry Office at Mammoth (307/344-2160 or 307/344-2163), and at the ski shops at Old Faithful and Mammoth Hot Springs (307/344-7311). Individual maps each cover an area in the park. It's a good idea to check with a visitor center for current trail and weather conditions before you start. If researching ahead of your visit, you might review the Yellowstone Nation Park website (www.yellowstonenationalpark.com/skiing.htm) for both general information and trail descriptions; for detailed trail information, go to the Nordic Trails section of the Xanterra website (www.travelyellowstone.com).

Most trails are marked with orange metal markers attached to trees. But even on a well-marked trail it's easy to get lost in a whiteout or blizzard. Don't attempt off-trail ski travel unless you really know the area. Since all the unplowed roadways are also used by snowmobilers, skiers should travel facing traffic and stay alert, to avoid accidents. For more information on safety precautions for skiers in Yellowstone, see the *What do we need to know about skiing in the park?* section of this chapter.

Winter warming huts are located at several points of interest or major road junctions. These winterized trailers or small rustic cabins offer information and a welcome retreat from the cold. Most have food service, but Indian Creek does not. Vending machines dispense hot drinks and snacks at West Thumb and Fishing Bridge. Madison and Canyon offer a limited selection of both. Keep an eye out for our roving ranger-naturalists at the warming huts and at major features in the park.

Cross-country skiers can receive expert instruction and rent gear at the Bear Den ski shops at Old Faithful and Mammoth Hot Springs. A ski package, including skis, poles, boots, and gaiters, costs $11 per person for a half day, $16 for a full day. If you add a group lesson, the package price is $30 per person for a full day. A two-hour group ski lesson runs $20 per person ($30 with equipment rental), or you can arrange for a private cross-country lesson—the cost depends on length of time and equipment. There are also ski/lodging packages. For details and prices, contact Xanterra Parks & Resorts (307/344-7311 or 866/439-7375, www.travelyellowstone.com).

Ski shuttles run daily from both Old Faithful and Mammoth Hot Springs, taking skiers to Yellowstone's backcountry trails. On Fridays, from the end of December through the end of February, you can join a Cooke City See and Ski Tour departing from Mammoth for $68.50 per person; and on Saturdays, from the third week of December until the first of March, there are full-day Canyon Ski Tours departing from Mammoth for $118 per person. Contact Xanterra for schedules and information.

Here are some suggestions for easy trails (2–5 miles) that take you past some of the park's main features and most scenic areas. For others, check the trail maps for each area.

Canyon Area: Cascade Lake Trail, Canyon Rim Trail

Old Faithful Area: Lone Star Geyser Trail, Black Sand Basin Trail

Tower Area: Tower Falls Trail, Lost Lake Trail (between the trailhead and Lost Lake only), Chittenden Loop

Northeast Area: Bannock Trail, Barronette Trail

Mammoth Area: Sheepeater Trail, Indian Creek Loop, Bunsen Peak Trail (upper three miles only)

West Yellowstone: Riverside Ski Trails, Rendezvous Ski Trails, Gallatin National Forest

Northwest Corner from U.S. Highway 191: Telemark Meadow, milepost 18; Bighorn Pass Trail, milepost 20; Fawn Pass Trail, milepost 22; Specimen Creek Trail, milepost 27

Yellowstone's winter backcountry is wild, unpredictable, and vast. To make your wilderness experience a pleasant one, you'll need to take certain precautions before gliding into our backcountry areas. Here are some guidelines to help keep your trek worry-free:

- You'll need ski equipment that fits park conditions. Skis and boots must be made for touring or mountaineering. Narrow racing skis won't give you enough surface area to break trail, and low shoes won't give you enough ankle support for our mostly untracked backcountry trails. Snow may not pack down until February or March, so you may sink to the ground, even on skis or snowshoes, until late in the season.

- Because winter temperatures in Yellowstone are severe, proper clothes are important. It's best to be prepared for changing weather conditions by wearing several adjustable clothing layers. Remember, it's just as important to prevent overheating as it is to avoid chilling. For best results you should have a windproof, hooded outer layer, with wool or other insulating clothing underneath. Pants that block wind and rain are a good idea, and thick wool socks, gaiters, and overboots can help keep your feet warm and dry. Gloves or wool mittens with shells that breathe are important to allow moisture to escape from sweaty hands, and a facemask-style stocking cap or parka hood will help keep your head warm. Snow blindness and sunburn are always concerns, so don't forget sunglasses and sunscreen.

- When planning your trip, you need to allow for limited daylight (8:30 A.M.–5 P.M.), unpredictable snow conditions, and temperature extremes. Discuss your plans with a ranger at a visitor center, ranger station, or the Central Backcountry Office (307/344-2160 or 307/344-2163). Staff members in the ski shops at Mammoth and Old Faithful can help you choose the right gear for your trek. Plan your excursion so the weakest member of your group will enjoy and survive it, and be prepared to repair your equipment along the way.

For safety, follow these winter backcountry tips:

- Never closely approach geysers, hot springs, or mud pots. You can easily fall through the thin crusts that surround these areas. Snow turns to slippery ice around hot spots. Don't leave the designated trail in geothermal areas.

- Keep alert for icy conditions on downhill grades, especially those in thermal areas. Ski around icy areas or walk down the hill rather than risk skiing into a boiling pool.

- Beware of avalanche hazards, especially on hillsides or in canyons with steep slopes. Risks of avalanches can be high on roads between the east entrance and Fishing Bridge Junction, on Dunraven Pass, on trails in the Cooke City area, and even near Mammoth. Learn about safe travel methods and rescue procedures, and ask about trail conditions at a ski shop or visitor center.

- Be very cautious when crossing frozen lakes. Check ice thickness with your ski pole. Ice may be thin, especially near inlets, outlets, and waters warmed by thermal activity. River crossings can be dangerous. Ask a ranger about local crossings.

- Never approach wildlife. Animals are unpredictable, and, if they charge, you can't outrun them, especially in deep snow. In this environment, you and the animals need to conserve energy.

- Stay alert in burned areas. Fires create hazardous standing trees that can fall with little warning. Stay on designated trails.

- Carry adequate water, remembering that exertion in dry mountain air can dehydrate you. A good rule of thumb is to carry two quarts per person per day, plus gear to melt ice and purify water from streams, if necessary. Wrap a thermos in your sweater or down vest so your drink won't freeze.

- Carry more easy-to-eat food than you do in summer. By keeping fueled, you'll stay warmer and enjoy skiing more.

- Follow basic ski etiquette: Yield to those skiing downhill, and avoid hiking or snowshoeing in ski tracks.

- Cruising frozen crust in spring on skating skis can be exhilarating. Check conditions around April 1 with Freeheel and Wheel in West Yellowstone (406/646-7744).

Now, let's hit those beautiful trails!

What else is there to do in the winter besides ski?

Yellowstone is entirely different in winter from its summer character. There are fewer visitors and a shift in animals. Some migrate; others hibernate or retreat into winter survival mode. Nevertheless, winter is a marvelous time for wildlife viewing. Elk and bison are commonly seen in the Lamar, Pelican, and Hayden Valleys and along the Firehole River. But it's important to recognize that our animals must conserve their energy to survive the winter. Give them a wide berth, and, if they're walking toward your moving car or snowmobile, pull over to the side of the road opposite the animals and wait until they are completely past you before driving on. Wolves, restored to Yellowstone beginning in 1995, are frequently visible in the Lamar Valley. Stay on the road, and use good binoculars to see them. Trumpeter swans and Canada geese winter on the warmed rivers along the roads.

Guided snowmobile tours are a great way to see the park in winter. These full-day tours ($230 for one rider, $250 for two) depart from both Old Faithful Snow Lodge or Mammoth Hot Springs to visit the Canyon/Lake area. Or there is a daily trip from Old Faithful Lodge to Mammoth and trips from Mammoth to Old Faithful on Tuesday, Thursday, Saturday, and Sunday. Alternately, you may rent a snowmobile, or a fleet, plus hire a guide and chart your own expedition: Full-day guide services are $240; full-day snowmobile rental at Mammoth Hot Springs or Old Faithful is $185 for one rider or $200 for two riders. Children (11 and under) ride free with an adult.

Snow-coach touring in a heated, over-snow vehicle is one of the more comfortable ways to see the winter sights and learn interesting facts about the park. Tours are $64 for adults and $32 for children ages 2–11, and depart from Old Faithful Snow Lodge, Mammoth Hot Springs, West Yellowstone, and Flagg Ranch. There are also full or partial day interpretive tours leaving from Mammoth Hot Springs to the Grand Canyon, Norris Geyser Basin, or wildlife areas; adult and child prices vary depending on length of tour and destination. For information on any of these activities, contact Xanterra Parks & Resorts (307/344-7311 or 866/439-7375, www.travelyellowstone.com).

In addition to the services provided by Xanterra, visitors can find snow-coach operators, snowmobile operators, and cross-country guides and outfitters close to each park entrance through the National Park service website (www.nps.gov/yell/planyourvisit/wintbusn.htm).

Hearty campers can brave the cold at Mammoth, the only campground open in winter. To stay at any backcountry campsite, you must get a permit from a ranger station or call the Central Backcountry Office (307/344-2160 or 307/344-2163).

You can rent ice skates at the Mammoth Ski Shop and then whirl around the rink behind the Mammoth Hot Springs Hotel. Snowshoe rentals are also available at the ski shop, if you'd like to ramble along a snowy backcountry trail. Lodging is available at both the Mammoth Hot Springs Hotel and Old Faithful Snow Lodge, with evening ranger-naturalist programs at both locations. For reservations and information, contact Xanterra.

·The Future of Yellowstone·

Today, Yellowstone National Park is serving the needs of both recreation and science. Its pool of genetic diversity is allowing us to make a wealth of valuable new discoveries. The park offers unique opportunities for a better understanding of how the natural world works, from learning more about our wild animals' behaviors and diseases to tracking global climate changes, measuring increases in air and water pollution, and unlocking the secrets of genetic fingerprinting by studying the microorganisms in park hot springs. Yellowstone gives us a place of unparalleled beauty and bounty.

Just as the park has provided answers about how natural systems work, it has raised some serious questions about its ability to exist as an island of 2.2 million acres in the heart of an ecosystem that extends over 18 million acres, well beyond park boundaries.

The future of Yellowstone's wildlife and geothermal features are at the heart of the debate over park boundaries. Some of the park's migratory animals roam out of the park each winter to feed in low-lying valleys in national forests and on privately owned lands, where conflicts arise. Yellowstone fisheries and life forms inside the park can be compromised by resource development activities outside the park. Tapping into geothermal pools beyond park boundaries can change the delicate dynamics of Yellowstone's geysers and hot springs.

The solution will be found in our ability to understand how this vast ecosystem works. Increasing our knowledge about the Greater Yellowstone Ecosystem will enable us to make more intelligent decisions about the future of this amazing place called Yellowstone.

Ranger's Farewell

I hope that I've answered all of your questions about Yellowstone and that you've learned some inside information on ways to make your visit to the park more enjoyable.

The next chapter in the book is called *Quick Reference.* It's filled with lots of easy-to-find facts, forms, and information about the park. The subjects are in alphabetical order so you can quickly find what you need without having to thumb through the whole section. My favorite is the *Telephone and Website Directory,* which gives you numbers for everything I talked about in the book.

Good hunting, and be sure to let us know if we need to change anything to improve future editions of this handbook. You can write to:

Susan Frank
c/o Avalon Travel
1700 Fourth Street
Berkeley, CA 94710

Bye for now,
Ranger Norm

BEAR MANAGEMENT AREAS
IN YELLOWSTONE

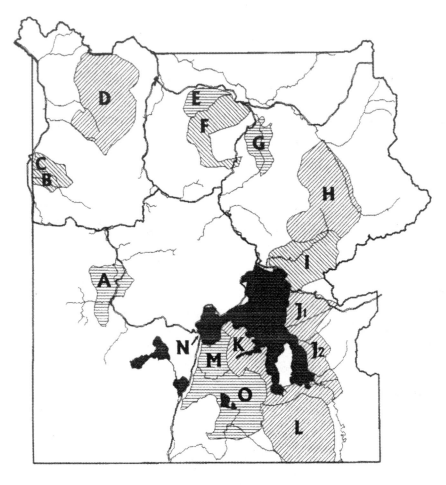

Lakes

Seasonally Restricted Areas

Seasonally Closed/Restricted Areas

Seasonally Closed Areas

Roads

Major Rivers

A: Firehole. This area (including Firehole Freight Road and Firehole Lake Road) is closed March 10 through the Friday of Memorial Day weekend. The Mary Mountain Trail from the Nez Perce trailhead to Mary Lake is closed March 10–June 15. Through travel from the Canyon trailhead is not allowed; however, travel is allowed from the Canyon trailhead to Mary Lake and back. Streamside use is allowed from the point where Nez Perce Creek crosses the main road to a point one mile upstream along Nez Perce Creek.

B: Richard's Pond. Area closed March 10 through the Friday of Memorial Day weekend. From the Saturday of Memorial Day weekend through September 30, Duck Creek, from the park boundary upstream to the Campanula Creek/Richard's Creek fork, is open to streamside travel. The area upstream from Campanula Creek/Richard's Creek fork is closed March 10–September 30.

C: Gneiss Creek. Area closed March 10–June 30. From July 1 through November 10, travel is allowed only on designated trails (off-trail travel is prohibited).

D: Gallatin. From May 1 through November 10, travel is allowed only on designated trails (off-trail travel is prohibited). A minimum group size of four is recommended for hiking and camping.

E: Blacktail. Area closed March 10–June 30.

F: Washburn. Area closed August 1–November 10. From March 10 through July 31, the area is open by special permit only. Contact the Tower Ranger Station for permit information.

G: Antelope. Area closed March 10–November 10. Dunraven Road and related turnouts are open. From May 25 through November 10, foot travel is allowed on the Old Road Trail from Tower Falls Campground to the Buffalo Picnic Area.

H: Mirror Plateau. From May 15 through November 10, the area is open to day use only, with the exception that July 1–August 14, overnight camping is permitted for a combined total of 14 nights per summer at the 3O1 and 5P7 campsites.

I: Pelican Valley. Area closed April 1–July 3. From July 4 through November 10, the area is open to day use only between the hours 9 A.M.–7 P.M.

J1: Clear Creek. From April 1 through August 10, travel is allowed only on the east shore from Nine-Mile trailhead to Park Point. All other trails are closed, and off-trail travel is prohibited. On August 11, all other campsites are open and off-trail travel is permitted.

J2: From April 1 through July 14, travel is allowed only on the east shore trail from Park Point to Beaverdam Creek. All other trails are closed; off-trail travel is prohibited. Open campsites are 5E2, 5E3, 5E4, 5E6, and 5H1 (no off-trail travel). All other campsites are closed. On July 15, all campsites are open and off-trail travel is permitted.

K: Lake Spawn. From May 15 through July 14, no off-trail travel is allowed; the trail between Cabin Creek and Outlet Creek is closed. Open campsites are 7L5, 7L6, 7L7, 7M3, 7M4, 6A3, and 6B1 (no travel away from campsite). On July 15, all campsites open and off-trail travel is permitted.

L: Two Ocean. From March 10 through July 14 and August 22 through November 10, travel is allowed only on designated trails (off-trail travel is prohibited). From July 15 through August 21, a permit is required for travel other than on designated trails. Contact the South Entrance Ranger Station for permit information.

M: Riddle/Solution. Area closed April 30–July 14.

N: Grant Village. Campground opens June 20 (earlier if bear use of the area spawning streams has ended before then). If bears are still frequenting the spawning stream after June 20, the campground loops adjacent to the stream will remain closed until bear activity ceases. Campground closes November 16.

O: Heart Lake. Area closed April 1–June 30.

BACKCOUNTRY REGULATIONS

The National Park Service is required by public law "to preserve" park resources and the values and purposes for which the park was established, as well as "to provide for the enjoyment" of those resources and values by such means as will leave them "unimpaired for future generations."

You can help us by obeying the following regulations:

- Camping outside designated sites is prohibited.
- Open fires are permitted only in established fire-rings at designated backcountry sites that allow wood fires. Only dead and down wood may be used as firewood.
- Food, garbage, cooking gear, and other odorous items must be suspended at least 10 feet above the ground at night and when unattended.
- Carry out your trash. If you pack it in, pack it out.
- Bury human waste at least 100 feet from a water source, campsite, or trail.
- Bathing, soaking, or swimming in water entirely of thermal origin is prohibited.
- Pets, weapons, or traps are prohibited in the backcountry.
- Tossing, throwing, or rolling rocks or other items inside caverns; into valleys, canyons, or caves; down hillsides or mountainsides; or into thermal features is prohibited.
- Bicycles, wheeled vehicles, and operating motorized equipment in the backcountry are prohibited.
- Feeding or intentionally disturbing wildlife is prohibited.
- Collecting or disturbing natural features, plants, rocks, antlers, cultural, or archaeological resources is prohibited.
- Only certified weed-free feed and grain may be taken into the backcountry. Hay is prohibited in the backcountry.
- Picketed animals shall not be kept within 100 feet of trails, campsites, or water sources.
- Stock manure shall be scattered in meadows and removed from within or near campsites.
- Tying stock to any living or dead feature causing injury or damage to the feature, vegetation, or soil is prohibited.
- Pack strings are not permitted to travel off-trail unless no other access is available to a designated camp area.
- Impeding or disturbing horses or pack animals is prohibited.

CHRONOLOGY OF YELLOWSTONE'S HISTORIC EVENTS

1797	A map of unknown authorship referred to the *"R. des Roches Jaunes"*—"Yellow Stone" in English.
1807	John Colter was the first white person to see what is now the national park. He probably saw some hot springs but no geysers.
1825	Mountain men began to hunt, trap, and trade in the area. Their accounts of the thermal wonders were mostly considered "tall tales."
1829	Fort Floyd (later Fort Union) was built at the mouth of the Yellowstone River by the American Fur Company.
1833	Manuel Alvarez led American Fur Company trappers across the Yellowstone Plateau and discovered the great geysers of the Firehole River basins.
1840	Fur trading as an organized business ended in the northern Rocky Mountains.
1843	Jim Bridger, a former trapper, built a way station on the Oregon Trail (Fort Bridger), from which he guided travelers through Yellowstone country.
1862	John White struck gold at Grasshopper Creek on the Yellowstone Plateau.
1863	"Colonel" Walter Washington deLacy explored the Snake River to its source. He published his *Map of the Territory of Montana with Portions of the Adjoining Territories*, which showed a "Hot Spring Valley" (the Firehole geyser basins) at the head of an unnamed lake draining southward into "Jackson's Lake."
1867	Surveyor General Meredith of Montana Territory identified the unnamed Lake deLacy. The name was later changed to Shoshone Lake by Professor Frank H. Bradley of Hayden's geological survey.
1868	An unratified treaty was used as justification for placing all the Shoshone Indians on small reservations.
1870	General H. D. Washburn's expedition undertook a definitive exploration of Yellowstone, observing and naming important features and perhaps giving early impetus to the idea of creating a national park.
1871	A government expedition headed by Dr. Ferdinand V. Hayden surveyed the park. The images created by painter Thomas Moran and

photographer William H. Jackson powerfully conveyed the natural wonders of Yellowstone.

1872   Influenced by Dr. Hayden's report, Congress passed S 392; President Ulysses S. Grant signed it into law on March 1, making Yellowstone the first national park.

1877–1882 Park superintendent Philetus W. Norris recommended hiring a gamekeeper. This task eventually grew into the first federal game management program. Norris pioneered park roads to principal features and extended existing trails.

1877   The Nez Perce Indians traversed the park during their long, desperate, and doomed flight toward Canada; in the park they skirmished with whites and kidnapped some tourists.

1878   The Bannock War spilled over into the park. Bannock Indians were attacked by 35 soldiers and 75 Crow scouts. Nine Bannock and two attackers were killed. It was the last Indian-Anglo armed conflict in Yellowstone.

1879   Anticipating trouble with the Bannock Indians, Superintendent Norris picked an easily defensible site for construction of park headquarters. This was the Norris blockhouse on Capitol Hill in Mammoth Hot Springs.

1883   The National Hotel was erected at Mammoth Hot Springs—a 3–4-story frame building, 414 feet long and 54 feet wide. Three tent hotels were operated by the Yellowstone Park Improvement Company at Norris Geyser Basin, the Grand Canyon of the Yellowstone, and the Upper Geyser Basin.

1886   The failure of Congress to provide funds for the administration of Yellowstone left park administrators without means for effective management. The secretary of the interior had no alternative but to fall back upon a provision of the Sundry Civil Act of 1883, which authorized him to call upon the secretary of war for assistance. This marked the end of civilian administration of the park. Former assistant superintendent "Yellowstone Jack" Baronett stayed on as a scout for the soldiers—the first of the legendary mountaineers who served as the army's "eyes" in the wilderness.

1886   Captain Moses Harris brought 50 men of the First U.S. Cavalry from Fort Custer, in the Montana Territory, to Mammoth Hot Springs. Harris assumed the duties of superintendent on August 20, and the army took over administration of the park.

1888   Over a hundred blazes originated in the park, some of them caused by lightning. The soldiers fought the fires so competently that fewer than five acres of timber were destroyed.

1889   The Canyon Hotel was completed.

1891   The Yellowstone Park Association opened the Fountain Hotel in the geyser basin. The first wing of the Lake Yellowstone Hotel was completed, with 80 rooms. (A 1903 addition to the Lake Hotel brought the building's total to 160 guest rooms.)

1891   The government decided to retain the army's management of the park. Fort Yellowstone was established, with permanent facilities to replace the temporary structures of Camp Sheridan.

1902   The Yellowstone domestic buffalo herd was established.

1902   The first automobile entered Yellowstone National Park.

1903   The Gateway Arch at the north entrance to the park was built, and President Theodore Roosevelt dedicated it. The East Entrance Road was opened to traffic.

1904   Old Faithful Inn, said to be the largest log structure in the world, opened.

1915   Automobiles were admitted into the park on a regular basis. A Ford Model T roadster received permit no. 1.

1916   Free auto camps were built at Mammoth Hot Springs, Old Faithful, Lake, and Canyon, probably the earliest attempt to provide for the needs of the new automobile travelers.

1918   The National Park Service took over park administration from the army.

1919   Horace M. Albright became the first Yellowstone superintendent under the National Park Service. He served until 1929.

1921   Auto camps opened at Lake and Fishing Bridge. The Old Faithful and Canyon Ranger Stations were completed.

1924   The Canyon auto campground opened. Covering 30 acres, it had full facilities and served 14,923 people in its first 52-day season.

1936   The Yellowstone Park Company was established as an amalgam of hotel, transportation, boat, lodging, and fuel companies.

1943   A B-17 bomber crashed in the park, killing 10 of the 11 airmen aboard.

1943–1945 During World War II, gasoline and tire rationing restricted park travel to occasional visits by local people and the few cross-country travelers allowed to use their automobiles for business or for changing residences.

1946   A wave of visitors, almost twice the size of peak visitation before the war, inundated the park.

1953   Charles Ashworth Hamilton purchased the unique refreshment stand on the upper terraces called the Devil's Kitchenette. His heirs purchased other interests after his death in 1957.

1955   The first evidence of the presence of Early Hunters was discovered—a Hell Gap point found at Nez Perce Creek within the Lower Geyser Basin.

1955   The NPS established "Mission 66," a broad program to accommodate thousands of visitors by 1966 without damage to the park. Turnouts would allow visitors to stop and enjoy scenery, picnic, and fish. Sections of old road would be turned into scenic loops. Older cabin accommodations would be replaced with motel-type units, increasing capacity from 8,500 to 14,500 people. The number of stores, filling stations, and eating establishments would increase, and employee facilities would be improved.

1959   Canyon Hotel, with all its furnishings, was sold to wreckers for $25.

1959   Frank and John Craighead began their grizzly bear research in the park.

1970   As part of an intensive bear management program, the last of the open garbage dumps was closed.

1976   Yellowstone National Park was designated a U.S. Biosphere Reserve.

1978   The park was accepted as a World Heritage Site.

1988   Wildfires—some caused by humans, some by nature—burned about a third of the total acreage of the park. The huge conflagrations led to much public questioning of the park's natural-fire policy. Many scientists took advantage of the event to study the effects of large wildland fires.

1990   State and federal agencies began work on a bison management plan.

1994   Fires burned more than 16,000 acres inside the park.

1995   Gray wolves were reintroduced into Yellowstone National Park after an absence of more than 50 years.

1998   Ten years after the huge fires of 1988, the regeneration of forests and animal habitats was evident throughout Yellowstone.

EDUCATIONAL PROGRAMS AND FACILITIES

Yellowstone Association Institute Programs

The Yellowstone Association Institute (P.O. Box 117, Yellowstone National Park, WY 82190, 307/344-2293, www.yellowstoneassociation.org) offers in-depth educational programs to the public. Based at the historic Buffalo Ranch in the Lamar Valley, the institute conducts almost a hundred multiple-day courses on such subjects as wildflowers, grizzly bear and wolf ecology, birds, geology, photography, writing and art, fly fishing, and history. It also offers a variety of backcountry courses about alpine flowers, bear safety, geology, and history. Llamas and horses are used for most of the backcountry courses. Winter courses address winter ecology, wilderness search and rescue, and snow tracking. Families and children can participate in courses and nature study vacations designed especially for them. The institute offers about a third of its courses for college credit.

Teton Science School Programs

Since 1967, Teton Science School (P.O. Box 68, Kelly, WY 83011, 307/733-4765, www.tetonscience.org) has been an important resource for educating, training, and inspiring students of all ages in natural science and ecology while fostering an appreciation for conservation ethics and practices. From a 40-acre campus in Grand Teton National Park, TSS operates its year-round residential and nonresidential programs. The Greater Yellowstone Area (including Yellowstone National Park) serves as an outdoor classroom. Throughout the year, elementary, junior high, and high school students participate in residential natural science field courses, while adults have access to teacher workshops, natural history seminars, Elderhostel programs, and custom adult programs. TSS teaches natural science and field studies to public school teachers and students in Wyoming, Montana, and Idaho. A one-year academic program trains college graduate students in teaching, developing, and managing environmental educational programs.

Educational Exhibits in Yellowstone National Park

In addition to exhibits at the five visitor centers inside the park, the **Museum of the National Park Ranger** (307/344-7353, late May–early Sept. daily 9 A.M.–6 P.M.), in Norris has educational exhibits you may enjoy. The museum traces the development of the park ranger from soldier to modern specialist. A history video is shown daily. The **Norris Geyser Basin Museum** (307/344-2812, late May–early Sept. daily 8 A.M.–7 P.M.) is a great place to view exhibits and learn more about the park's geothermal features.

Educational Exhibits in the Greater Yellowstone Area

Five museums within a half-day's drive of Yellowstone's boundaries provide educational opportunities for a deeper understanding and knowledge of the park. The **Buffalo Bill Historical Center** (307/587-4771) in Cody, Wyoming, tells the story of the early humans in the area and, in its Whitney Gallery of Western Art, gives visitors an artistic interpretation of Yellowstone's landscape and unusual features. Exhibits at the **Museum of the Rockies** (406/994-2251) in Bozeman, Montana, tell the story of the Greater Yellowstone Ecosystem through fascinating paleontology and geology displays and interactive activities. The museum also houses the area's only planetarium. At the **National Wildlife Art Museum** (307/733-5771) in Jackson, Wyoming, park visitors can see Yellowstone wildlife beautifully depicted in a variety of media, including bronze, oils, and acrylics. The **Museum of the Mountain Man** (307/367-4101), located in Pinedale, Wyoming, has exhibits that examine the life of Jim Bridger, one of the first Euro-Americans to visit Yellowstone, and that tell the story of other early explorers, mountain men, and fur trappers. At the **National Bighorn Sheep Interpretive Center** (307/455-3429) in Dubois, Wyoming, you'll see exhibits highlighting the habitat, predator–prey relationships, lambing, and dominance behaviors of the area's bighorn sheep.

Interpretive Programs

National Park Service interpretive programs of many types and covering a wide range of subjects are offered both day and night in the park. Included are films, campfire programs, and special ranger walks and talks. Check *Yellowstone Today* for schedule and details, or call one of the visitor centers.

Xanterra Parks & Resorts (307/344-7311 or 866/439-7375, www.travel yellowstone.com) also offers interpretive programs, including narrated motorcoach sightseeing tours, narrated scenic-cruiser rides around Yellowstone Lake, and free historic walking tours of the Lake Yellowstone Hotel and the Old Faithful Inn.

FAMILY ATTRACTIONS

Explore with interactive books. The Yellowstone Association (307/344-2293, www.yellowstoneassociation.org) has some great books for kids who want to explore the park. *The World of Small* comes with a magnifying lens to teach kids how "big" small things can become. *The Kids' Wildlife Book* introduces children to the park's wonderful animal population with over a hundred learning experiences using science, language arts, nature, math, and arts and crafts. Yellowstone Association bookstores are located throughout the park, and books are on sale through the website as well.

Hike a fire trail built by kids. East of Mammoth Hot Springs, you can walk along a 0.5-mile boardwalk that meanders through an area burned during the 1988 fires. Five interpretive stations encourage visitors to get down on their hands and knees to look for lush new growth emerging amid the blackened trees. Built by classes of local schoolchildren to teach kids about the effects and ecology of fire, the trail was completely renovated in 1997. Contact the Yellowstone Association (307/344-2263), or visit the Albright Visitor Center for more information.

Become a tour guide. Kids love to operate the self-guided auto audio tour rental units available at most hotel activity desks. The tour makes learning about the park fun and entertaining, with stories and songs for the whole family. Check at hotel front or activity desks for more information or contact Xanterra (307/344-7311 or 866/439-7375, www.travelyellowstone.com).

Become a Junior Ranger. During the summer, you can pick up a *Junior Ranger* newspaper for $2 at any visitor center and start tracking animals, predicting geyser eruptions, and more. Kids 7–12 who complete enough activities earn Junior Ranger patches. The program runs early June–Labor Day.

Watch Old Faithful erupt. You won't want to miss this magnificent live show, which happens about every 1.3 hours. Contact the Old Faithful Visitor Center (307/545-2750) for more information and estimated eruption times.

Catch a fish. Kids can try their luck with a rod and reel aboard the guided fishing boats available at Bridge Bay Marina at Yellowstone Lake. Contact Xanterra (307/344-7311 or 866/439-7375, www.travelyellowstone.com) for more information.

Ride a stagecoach. You can catch a ride in a real horse-drawn stagecoach. Rides head out several times a day from Roosevelt Lodge at Tower-Roosevelt. For reservations and information, contact Xanterra (307/344-7311 or 866/439-7375, www.travelyellowstone.com), or ask at lodging activity desks throughout the park.

Come to a western-style cookout. You can enjoy a meal the way the pioneers did, over an open campfire. Cookouts are offered daily by Roosevelt Lodge June–Labor Day and include great grub and western entertainment for the whole family. Contact Xanterra (307/344-7311 or 866/439-7375, www.travelyellowstone.com) for reservations and information.

Attend a campfire program. At family campfire programs you'll hear tales about mountain men and Native Americans along with stories about bison, elk, and bear. Check *Yellowstone Today* or ask at any visitor center for program times and locations.

Join a ranger-led activity. A host of ranger-led activities are specially designed for young visitors to Yellowstone. Fun educational films are also shown daily at several visitor centers, and most visitor centers have kid-friendly exhibits. At Albright Visitor Center in Mammoth, for example, the animal displays and trapper exhibit delight kids. Check times and locations of ranger-led activities in *Yellowstone Today*, or ask at any visitor center.

Enjoy a kid discount. Kids 11 and under stay free at park lodges, and most activities, services, and tours offer discounts for young visitors. Contact Xanterra (307/344-7311 or 866/439-7375, www.travelyellowstone.com), or stop at lodging front or activity desks.

HISTORIC PEOPLE AND EVENTS

The Hayden Survey of 1871

While no one person can claim credit for Yellowstone National Park's creation, Ferdinand V. Hayden, director of the U.S. Geological Society, played a major role in the park's 1872 establishment. A surgeon during the Civil War, Dr. Hayden had the scientific training and lifelong interest in geology that enabled him to launch an expedition, designated "United States Geological Survey of the Territories" by the secretary of the interior, in 1869. With an appropriation of $40,000, Hayden set out in 1871 to explore the Yellowstone area. His 34-man expedition included a young landscape painter, Thomas Moran, and a photographer, William Henry Jackson. These two proved important: Moran's paintings and Jackson's photographs revealed a region of stunning beauty. Their pictures and the 500-page survey report gave irrefutable evidence that the thermal features and other natural wonders of the Yellowstone Plateau existed and deserved to be protected. Based in large part on Hayden's survey, Yellowstone National Park was formally established on March 1, 1872.

The Nez Perce War of 1877

When the U.S. government tried to force the Nez Perce people of Chief Joseph onto an Idaho reservation to free their land for settlers, war erupted. Rather than face army reinforcements, 1,000 Nez Perce began a desperate 1,800-mile flight to Canada. After a series of battles, the Nez Perce entered Yellowstone from the west. They attacked tourists and prospectors; two whites were killed in the park, others were kidnapped, and one man nearly died from his wounds. Two weeks later, the Nez Perce exited the park to the east, escaping two columns of soldiers by heading north up the narrow Clarks Fork Canyon. Finally, near the Canadian border, the army caught up with the tribe and forced it to surrender, although 300 Nez Perce escaped into Canada. Yellowstone's Nez Perce Creek is named for this historic bid for freedom.

Collins Jack Baronett

"Yellowstone Jack" was a sailor, soldier, miner, and guide. Baronett came to the Montana Territory as a prospector in 1864 and lived long enough around the Yellowstone country to earn his nickname. He entered Yellowstone with the expedition of 1866, and served as a scout with General Custer's expedition to the Black Hills and with another Yellowstone expedition in 1869. Baronett conducted the successful search for Truman Everts, who was lost for 37 days in Yellowstone during the 1870 expedition of the area. "Yellowstone Jack" operated a toll bridge over the Yellowstone River as a vital link in the road to the mining area on Clarks Fork until 1894. Baronett was the preferred guide of General Philip H. Sheridan and the only member of the original civilian police force to be retained by the army when it took over park management in 1886. His 35-year association with the park is commemorated by Baronett Peak, which flanks the Northeast Entrance Road.

Philetus W. Norris

The second superintendent of Yellowstone National Park was a pioneer and a scientist. Philetus W. Norris was responsible for building the first trails, roads, and buildings in the park, as well as recording the area's human and natural history. He had served as a senator in the Ohio legislature and built successful real estate and newspaper businesses, which gave him the resources to make many expeditions through the West. On a trip through the new park in 1875, Norris wrote newspaper articles about the shortcomings of the first Yellowstone superintendent, Nathaniel P. Langford. As a result, Norris was named superintendent on April 18, 1877, and served until 1882. He helped open Yellowstone to visitors, secured the first federal appropriations for improvements to the park, and built the Mammoth–Norris Road to the geyser basins and the first park headquarters building at Mammoth. His explorations and prolific writing helped popularize the park for the first tourists and contributed to the study of ethnology, archaeology, and geology in the area.

Horace M. Albright

Albright was superintendent of Yellowstone National Park 1919–1929. He had played an important role in passage of the legislation creating the National Park Service in 1916, and he had served as assistant director of the new NPS. During his tenure as park superintendent, roads were rebuilt to accommodate automobile traffic into the park, campgrounds were developed, interpretive services were established, and concessionaires were encouraged to provide a full range of visitor services. Albright also helped preserve park wildlands by preventing water and power interests from encroaching on the park. He promoted the establishment of Grand Teton National Park, which helped preserve crucial wilderness in the Yellowstone area. Perhaps his greatest achievement was the expansion of the NPS to include all federal historic sites and structures and the park system of the District of Columbia. His legacy in Yellowstone is remembered with the Horace M. Albright Visitor Center at Fort Yellowstone in Mammoth Hot Springs.

LICENSED TOUR OPERATORS AND OUTFITTERS

BACKPACKING

Big Wild Adventures
Emigrant, MT
406/848-7000
www.bigwildadventures.com

Bud Lilly's Trout Shop
West Yellowstone, MT
406/646-7801 or 800/854-9559
www.budlillys.com

Fatboy Fishing
Wilson, WY
307/733-3061

Greater Yellowstone Flyfishers
Bozeman, MT
406/586-2489
www.gyflyfishers.com

Hawkridge Outfitters
Bozeman, MT
406/585-9608

High Country Outfitters
Pray, MT
406/333-4763
www.highcountryoutfitters.com

Menogyn
Minneapolis, MN
612/823-5282

Montana Outdoor Adventures Inc.
West Yellowstone, MT
406/646-0059

National Outdoor Leadership Schools
Lander, WY
307/332-6973
www.nols.edu

Outpost Wilderness Adventures
Lake George, CO
719/748-3080
www.owa.com

Overland Travel, Inc.
Williamstown, MA
413/458-9672
www.overlandsummers.com

Rendezvous Outfitters/ Yellowstone Rough Riders
Gardiner, MT
406/848-7967 or 800/565-7110
www.yellowstoneroughriders.com

Sun Valley Trekking Company
Sun Valley, ID
208/788-1966
www.svtrek.com

Wilderness Alternative Schools
Marion, MT
406/854-2832

Wilderness Inquiry
Minneapolis, MN
612/676-9400
www.wildernessinquiry.org

Wilderness Institute
Livingston, MT
406/243-5361

Wilderness Ventures
Jackson, WY
307/733-2122
www.wildernessventures.com

Yellowstone Association
Yellowstone NP, WY
307/344-2293
www.yellowstoneassociation.org

Yellowstone Guidelines
Bozeman, MT
800/314-4506

Yellowstone Outfitters
Emigrant, MT
406/848-7755

BICYCLING
Adventure Cycling Association
Missoula, MT
406/721-1776
www.adv-cycling.org

Backcountry Bicycle Tours
Bozeman, MT
406/586-3556

Backroads, Inc.
Berkeley, CA
510/527-1555
www.backroads.com

Cycle America
Cannon Falls, MN
800/983-3263
www.cycleamerica.com

A Personal Guide Service
Jackson, WY
307/733-6312

Teton Mountain Bike Tours
Jackson, WY
307/733-2122
www.tetonmtbike.com

Timberline Adventures
Denver, CO
303/368-4418 or 800/417-2453
www.timbertours.com

Wilderness Ventures
Jackson, WY
307/733-2122
www.wildernessventures.com

CANOEING
Experience Montana
Sheridan, MT
406/842-5134

**Far and Away Adventures/
Paddle Yellowstone**
Sun Valley, ID
208/726-8888
www.far-away.com

**Snake River Kayak
and Canoe School**
Jackson, WY
307/733-9999 or 800/529-2501
www.snakeriverkayak.com

Sun Valley Trekking Company
Sun Valley, ID
208/788-1966
www.svtrek.com

Whitewater Sports
West Jordan, UT
801/280-2295

Wilderness Inquiry
Minneapolis, MN
612/676-9400
www.wildernessinquiry.org

Wilderness Ventures
Jackson, WY
307/733-2122
www.wildernessventures.com

DAY HIKING
Backcountry Bicycle Tours
Bozeman, MT
406/586-3556

Backroads, Inc.
Berkeley, CA
510/527-1555
www.backroads.com

**Far and Away Adventures/
Paddle Yellowstone**
Sun Valley, ID
208/726-8888
www.far-away.com

Grub Steak Expeditions
Cody, WY
307/527-6316
www.grubsteaktours.com

Lone Mountain Ranch
Big Sky, MT
406/995-4644 or 800/514-1844
www.lmranch.com

Madison River Outfitters
West Yellowstone, MT
406/646-9644
www.flyfishingyellowstone.com

Off the Beaten Path
Bozeman, MT
406/586-1311
www.offthebeatenpath.com

Overland Travel, Inc.
Williamstown, MA
413/458-9672
www.overlandsummers.com

A Personal Guide Service
Jackson, WY
307/733-6312

Rein Teen Tours, Inc.
Wayne, NJ
800/831-1313
www.reinteentours.com

Sierra Safaris International
Livingston, MT
406/222-8557

Trailside Productions
Bozeman, MT
406/995-4688

Wildlife Expeditions
Jackson, WY
307/733-2623 or 888/945-3567
www.wildlifeexpeditions.org

Yellowstone Day Hikes
West Yellowstone, MT
406/646-7242

Yellowstone/Glacier Adventures
Bozeman, MT
406/585-9041
www.national-park-tours.com

FISHING
Arrick's Fly Shop
West Yellowstone, MT
406/646-7290
www.arricks.com

Blue Ribbon Fishing Tours
Livingston, MT
406/369-0991 or 406/222-7714

Blue Ribbon Flies
West Yellowstone, MT
406/646-9365
www.blueribbonflies.com

Bressler Outfitters, Inc.
Wilson, WY
307/733-6934

Bud Lilly's Trout Shop
West Yellowstone, MT
406/646-7801 or 800/854-9559
www.budlillys.com

Eagle Creek Outfitters
Bozeman, MT
406/468-9171
www.eaglecreekoutfitters.net

East Slope Anglers
Big Sky, MT
406/995-4369
www.eastslopeoutdoors.com

Experience Montana
Sheridan, MT
406/842-5134

Far and Away Adventures/
Paddle Yellowstone
Sun Valley, ID
208/726-8888
www.far-away.com

Fatboy Fishing
Wilson, WY
307/733-3061

Firehole Ranch
West Yellowstone, MT
406/646-7294
www.fireholeranch.com

Gallatin River Guides
Big Sky, MT
406/995-2290
www.montanaflyfishing.com

Gary Evans, Madison River Guides
Rexburg, ID
406/581-3498
www.garyevansmadison-
riverguides.com

Greater Yellowstone Flyfishers
Bozeman, MT
406/586-2489
www.gyflyfishers.com

Grub Steak Expeditions
Cody, WY
307/527-6316
www.grubsteaktours.com

Hatch Finders
Livingston, MT
406/222-0989
www.hatchfinders.com

Hawkridge Outfitters
Bozeman, MT
406/585-9608

Headwaters Guide Service
Gallatin Gateway, MT
406/763-4761
www.headwatersguideservice.com

Henry's Fork Anglers
St. Anthony, ID
208/558-7525
www.henrysforkanglers.com

High Country Outfitters
Pray, MT
406/333-4763
www.highcountryoutfitters.com

Jacklin's, Inc.
West Yellowstone, MT
406/646-7336

John Henry Lee Outfitters, Inc.
Dubois, WY
307/455-3200 or 800/352-2576
www.johnhenrylee.com

Last Chance Outfitters
Island Park, ID
208/558-7068

Lee Watson Outfitter
Livingston, MT
406/333-4054

Lone Mountain Ranch
Big Sky, MT
406/995-4644 or 800/514-4844
www.lmranch.com

Lost River Outfitters
Ketchum, ID
208/726-1706
www.lostriveroutfitters.com

Madison River Outfitters
West Yellowstone, MT
406/646-9644
www.flyfishingyellowstone.com

Montana Outdoor Adventures, Inc.
West Yellowstone, MT
406/646-0059

Montana's Master Angler
Livingston, MT
406/222-2273

Outpost Wilderness Adventures
Lake George, CO
719/748-3080
www.owa.com

Overland Travel, Inc.
Williamstown, MA
413/458-9672
www.overlandsummers.com

Parks' Fly Shop
Gardiner, MT
406/848-7314
www.parksflyshop.com

Rendezvous Outfitters/ Yellowstone Rough Riders
Gardiner, MT
406/848-7967 or 800/565-7110
www.yellowstoneroughriders.com

The River's Edge
Bozeman, MT
406/586-5373
www.theriversedge.com

Snake River Fishing Trips
Jackson, WY
307/733-3270

Snake River Kayak and Canoe School
Jackson, WY
307/733-9999 or 800/529-2501
www.snakeriverkayak.com

Teton Troutfitters
Wilson, WY
307/733-5362
www.tetontroutfitters.com

Three Rivers Ranch
Ashton, ID
208/652-3750
www.threeriversranch.com

Tom Miner Lodge
Ismay, MT
406/772-5550

Triangle X Ranch
Moose, WY 83012
307/733-2183
www.trianglex.com

Westbank Anglers
Teton Village, WY
307/733-6483 or 800/922-3474
www.westbank.com

Wilderness Inquiry
Minneapolis, MN
612/676-9400
www.wildernessinquiry.org

Wild Trout Outfitters/ Mountain Taxi
Big Sky, MT
406/995-4895 or 800/423-4742
www.wildtroutoutfitters.com

Williams Guide Service
Livingston, MT
406/222-1386

Yellowstone Angler
Livingston, MT
406/222-7130
www.yellowstoneangler.com

Yellowstone Association
Yellowstone NP, WY
307/344-2293
www.yellowstoneassociation.org

Yellowstone/Glacier Adventures
Bozeman, MT
406/585-9041
www.national-park-tours.com

Yellowstone Outfitters
Emigrant, MT
406/848-7755

KAYAKING
**Far and Away Adventures/
Paddle Yellowstone**
Sun Valley, ID
208/726-8888
www.far-away.com

**Jackson Hole Kayak School/
Rendezvous River Sports**
Jackson, WY
307/733-2471
www.jacksonholekayak.com

OARS
Angels Camp, CA
209/736-4677
www.oars.com

Snake River Kayak and Canoe School
Jackson, WY
307/733-9999 or 800/529-2501
www.snakeriverkayak.com

Sun Valley Trekking Company
Sun Valley, ID
208/788-1966
www.svtrek.com

NATURAL HISTORY
A Naturalist's World
Gardiner, MT
406/848-9458
www.tracknature.com

Sandra Nykerk Photography
Gardiner, MT
406/848-7749 ·
www.sandranykerk.com

Wildlife Expeditions
Jackson, WY
307/733-2623 or 888/945-3567
www.wildlifeexpeditions.org

PHOTOGRAPHY
A Naturalist's World
Gardiner, MT
406/848-9458
www.tracknature.com

Dramatic Light Nature Photography
Grand Junction, CO
800/207-4686
www.dramaticlightphoto.com

Grub Steak Expeditions
Cody, WY
307/527-6316
www.grubsteaktours.com

Joseph Van Os Photo Safaris
Vashon Island, WA
206/463-5383
www.photosafaris.com

Lone Mountain Ranch
Big Sky, MT
406/995-4644 or 800/514-4844
www.lmranch.com

McDonald Wildlife Photography
McClure, PA
717/543-6423
www.hoothollow.com

Sandra Nykerk Photography
Gardiner, MT
406/848-7749
www.sandranykerk.com

Sierra Safaris International
Livingston, MT
406/222-8557

63 Ranch
Livingston, MT
888/395-5151
www.sixtythree.com

Teton Troutfitters
Wilson, WY
307/733-5362
www.tetontroutfitters.com

Trailside Productions
Bozeman, MT
406/995-4688

**Wilderness Photography
Expeditions**
Livingston, MT
406/222-2302
www.tmurphywild.com

Yellowstone Arctic/Yamaha
West Yellowstone, MT
406/646-9636
www.yellowstonearcticyamaha.com

Yellowstone/Glacier Adventures
Bozeman, MT
406/585-9041
www.national-park-tours.com

STOCK OUTFITTERS
Beardsley Outfitting
Ennis, MT
406/682-7292
www.beardsleyfishhuntmt.com

Bear Paw Outfitters
Livingston, MT
406/222-6642
www.bearpawoutfittersmt.com

Black Otter Guide Service
Pray, MT
406/333-4362
www.blackotterguideservice.com

Castle Creek Outfitters
Silver Gate, MT
406/838-2301

Covered Wagon Ranch
Gallatin Gateway, MT
800/995-4237
www.coveredwagonranch.com

Elkhorn Ranch
Gallatin Gateway, MT
406/995-4291
www.elkhornranchmt.com

Gary Fales Outfitting
Cody, WY
307/587-3747

Grizzly Ranch
Cody, WY
307/587-3966

Gunsel Horse Adventures
Rapid City, SD
605/343-7608
www.gunselhorseadventures.com

Hell's a Roarin'
Gardiner, MT
406/848-7578
www.hellsaroarinoutfitters.com

Jackson Hole Llamas
Jackson, WY
307/739-9582
www.jhllamas.com

Jake's Horses
Gallatin Gateway, MT
406/995-4630
www.jakeshorses.com

John Henry Lee Outfitters, Inc.
Dubois, WY
307/455-3200 or 800/352-2576
www.johnhenrylee.com

K Bar Z Guest Ranch
Cody, WY
307/587-4410
www.agonline.com/KBarZ

Llamas of West Yellowstone
Bozeman, MT
406/587-2661
www.llamasofwestyellowstone.com

Lone Mountain Ranch
Big Sky, MT
406/995-4644 or 800/514-4844
www.lmranch.com

Medicine Lake Outfitters
Bozeman, MT
406/388-4938
www.packtrips.com

Nine Quarter Circle Ranch
Gallatin Gateway, MT
406/995-4276
www.ninequartercircle.com

Rendezvous Outfitters/
Yellowstone Rough Riders
Gardiner, MT
406/848-7967 or 800/565-7110
www.yellowstoneroughriders.com

Ron Dube's Wilderness Adventures
Wapiti, WY
307/527-7815

7D Ranch
Cody, WY
307/587-9885
www.7dranch.com

Sheep Mesa Outfitters
Cody, WY
307/587-4305
www.sheepmesaoutfitters.com

Skyline Guest Ranch
Cooke City, MT
877/238-8885
www.flyfishyellowstone.com

Slough Creek Outfitters
North Livingston, MT
406/222-2734
www.sloughcreek.com

Teton Ridge Ranch
Tetonia, ID
208/456-2650 or 800/926-3579
www.tetonridge.com

T Lazy T Outfitters
Jackson, WY
307/733-4481
www.tlazytoutfitters.com

Triangle X Ranch
Moose, WY
307/733-2183
www.trianglex.com

Triple Tree Ranch
Bozeman, MT
406/587-1341

Two Ocean Pass Ranch/Outfitters
Moran, WY
307/543-2309
www.twooceanpass.com

Wilderness Trails
Jackson, WY
307/733-5171
www.wildernesstrailsinc.com

Wyoming Backcountry Adventures, Inc.
Powell, WY
307/754-4320

Yellowstone Llamas
Bozeman, MT
406/586-1155 or 866/586-1155
www.yellowstonesafari.com

TRANSPORTATION
Alltrans
Jackson, WY
307/733-3135 or 800/443-6133
www.jacksonholealltrans.com

Buffalo Bus Touring Company
West Yellowstone, MT
406/646-9353

Callowishus Park Touring Company
Jackson, WY
307/413-5483
www.callowishus.com

Crossed Sabres Ranch
Wapiti, WY
307/587-3750

Experience Montana
Sheridan, MT
406/842-5134

Grand Targhee Resort
Alta, WY
307/353-2300 or 800/827-4433
www.grandtarghee.com

Gray Line
Jackson Hole, WY
800/433-6133
www.graylinc.com

Green Tortoise, Inc.
San Francisco, CA
415/956-7500
www.greentortoise.com

Grub Steak Expeditions
Cody, WY
307/527-6316
www.grubsteaktours.com

Lone Mountain Ranch
Big Sky, MT
406/995-4644 or 800/514-4844
www.lmranch.com

Mountain Sky Guest Ranch
Emigrant, MT
800/548-3392
www.mtnsky.com

Northwest Passage/ Silver Eagle Shuttle
Billings, MT
406/254-2900

Off the Beaten Path
Bozeman, MT
406/586-1311
www.offthebeatenpath.com

Outdoor Adventures
Jackson, WY
307/739-9443 or 800/642-8979
www.upstreamangiers.com

A Personal Guide Service
Jackson, WY
307/733-6312

Powder River
Transportation Services
Gillette, WY
307/682-0960
www.coachamerica.com

Rimrock Dude Ranch
Cody, WY
307/587-3970
www.rimrockranch.com

Rocky Mountain Ministries
Jackson, WY
307/733-4945

63 Ranch
Livingston, MT
888/395-5151
www.sixtythree.com

Teton Troutfitters
Wilson, WY
307/733-5362
www.tetontroutfitters.com

Tom Miner Lodge
Ismay, MT
406/772-5550

Trek America
Gardena, CA
800/873-5872
www.trekamerica.com

Triangle C Guest Ranch
Dubois, WY
800/661-4928
www.trianglec.com

Turpin Meadows Ranch
Moran, WY
307/543-2000 or 800/743-2496
www.turpinmeadow.com

Wild Trout Outfitters/
Mountain Taxi
Big Sky, MT
406/995-4895 or 800/423-4742
www.wildtroutoutfitters.com

Yellowstone Safari Company
Bozeman, MT
406/586-1155
www.yellowstonesafari.com

PLACE NAMES OF YELLOWSTONE

Excerpted from Yellowstone Place Names, *by Lee H. Whittlesey, Montana Historical Society Press, Helena, Montana, 1988.*

Absaroka Range: Stretching some 80 miles and reaching heights of 12,000 feet, this magnificent mountain range forms the eastern boundary of Yellowstone National Park. Absaroka was the name that the Crow Indians used when referring to themselves; it has been interpreted to mean "children of the large-beaked bird" and "sparrowhawk people," among other things.

Abyss Pool: Long admired for its ultramarine hue and transparent depths, this hot spring was named by Chief Park Naturalist C. M. Bauer in 1935.

Albright Falls: Formerly known as Batchelder Column Cascade, these falls were renamed for a pivotal Yellowstone personality in 1986. Horace Marden Albright, one of the chief architects of the National Park Service and Yellowstone's superintendent for 10 years, helped save this section of the park when he lobbied against flooding the Bechler River with an irrigation dam.

Alum Creek: Flowing into the Yellowstone River from the east, Alum Creek no doubt was so named by early hunters and prospectors because thermal springs dumping into it soured its water. Today it is called Broad Creek or Sour Creek. Many tall tales revolve around it; one tells of a fur trapper who rode across the creek only to find that his horse's hooves had shrunk to the size of a pony's!

Anemone Geyser: This active geyser was named around 1886 by geologist Walter Weed, probably for its resemblance to a sea creature or to a flower. In recent years the central vent has erupted every 3–8 minutes with a duration of 20–30 seconds and a height of 3–12 feet.

Angel Terrace: This long-dormant terrace of Mammoth Hot Springs was named around 1895, possibly by the photographer F. Jay Harness. It is suggested that the "purity of the deposit and the resulting snowy whiteness of the terraces" led him to give the terrace its heavenly name.

Arsenic Geyser: Although this active geyser carries a dangerous name, it contains no more arsenic than other springs of the area. It may have been the green scorodite particles in the waters that led geologist Arnold Hague to name it Arsenic Geyser in 1887.

Artemisia Geyser: Geologist Walter Weed misnamed this geyser "Artemisia Spring" in 1883 because of the "sage color of its deposits"; Artemisia is the Latin name for the type of sagebrush that grows in Yellowstone. Only later, in 1886, did geologists correctly identify this site, part of the Cascade Group in Upper Geyser Basin, as a geyser.

Artist Point: Located on the south rim of the Grand Canyon of the

Yellowstone River, Artist Point is the most famous of the canyon viewpoints. It was erroneously thought that this was the vantage point artist Thomas Moran used when creating his famous 1872 painting of the canyon. In fact, he made his sketches on the north side of the canyon at a place now called Moran Point.

Astringent Creek: Initially named "Lake Creek" because surveyors thought it came from White Lake, this creek was given its present name in 1886 by geologist Arnold Hague. He recorded in his field notebooks that the stream should be given a name "suggestive of its alum and iron waters or its numerous springs."

Atomizer Geyser: The fine water spray emitted by this geyser led tour operator G. L. Henderson to give it this name sometime around 1885–1888. Atomizer Geyser is in all probability the spring that the Hayden survey party had named "Restless Geyser" in 1878.

Bannock Ford: This ford on the Yellowstone River is one of the few crossings inside the park. The Great Bannock Trail, used by local native tribes, met the Yellowstone River here. The ford bears the name of the tribe, which lived southwest of Yellowstone and were closely related to the Shoshone.

Bannock Peak: Originally named Norris Mountain by Park Superintendent P. W. Norris, this peak received its present name in 1885 from members of the Hague U.S. Geological Survey party. It's possible that the survey team selected the name because of a raid and theft of 20 horses at this site by Bannocks. The name Bannock has been translated to mean "people from below" or "people from across the water," among other interpretations.

Bath Lake: It's hard to believe that this dry lake bed could have such an exciting past. In the early days of the park, nude bathing was allowed in the local springs, and Bath Lake was one of the more popular spots for women and men alike. There was so much trouble with nudity at Bath Lake that Captain Moses Harris of the U.S. army finally closed it to daytime bathing. Only in 1912 could both men and women bathe at the lake "provided they were properly dressed." The lake went dry in 1926; the 1959 earthquake revived it, but by 1984 it had dried up again.

Beaver Lake: Park Superintendent P. W. Norris named this lake, located at the foot of Obsidian Cliff, in 1878. He took the name from a story supposedly told by fur trapper Jim Bridger, a "famous legend of a lake with millions of beaver nearly impossible to kill because of their superior cuteness, with haunts and houses in inaccessible grottoes in the base of a glistening mountain of glass."

Beehive Geyser: Always a favorite with park visitors, although it has a history of being an irregular performer, the Beehive Geyser was named in 1870 by members of the Washburn survey, who made the first recorded sighting of it:

"on the east side of the Firehole River is a symmetrical cone resembling an old fashioned straw beehive with the top cut off."

Biscuit Basin: This basin, which houses many geysers and pools, received its current name during the late 1880s because knobby, geyserite formations that resemble biscuits are found around Sapphire Pool and Cauliflower Geyser. Unfortunately, many of the biscuits were destroyed by the Yellowstone earthquake of 1959.

Black Dragon's Caldron: This giant, black, seething mud pot in the Mud Volcano area came into existence sometime in February 1948 with a violent explosion that uprooted trees. Chief Park Naturalist David Condon named the mud pot for its color and the lashing, tonguelike agitation it displayed shortly after it developed.

Blood Geyser: A member of the Artist Paint Pots group of thermal springs, the Blood Geyser first appeared in a guidebook by W. W. Wylie in 1882. Herman Haupt, in his book Yellowstone National Park, observed that the geyser "throws a column of water through a stratum of red mud, which stains the water of the creek flowing from it and gives rise to the name."

Boiling River: At 6–9 feet wide and about 2 feet deep, Boiling River is the largest discharging hot spring in the park. Once home to a rheumatism "treatment center" called McGuirk's Medicinal Springs, run by settler Matthew McGuirk, the site was vacated in 1874 at the urging of the park superintendent.

Brickyard Hill: This low hill north of Clearwater Springs was mentioned as the Brickyard in army scout Felix Burgess's dairy as early as 1898. The name crept into local usage at about that time because brickmakers obtained clay here to make bricks for Fort Yellowstone chimneys.

Bridge Bay: A natural bay on Yellowstone Lake, southwest of the Lake Hotel, Bridge Bay was deepened in the early 1960s to be used as a marina. It was named in 1880 because of a natural bridge of stone near the bay and a stream nearby that had been named Bridge Creek.

Bunsen Peak: Many geologists believe that Bunsen Peak is the neck or stock of an ancient volcano related to the Absaroka volcanics. This 8,564-foot mountain was named by members of the second Hayden survey in honor of the eminent German physicist Robert Wilhelm Eberhard von Bunsen. Bunsen studied geysers in Iceland and was well respected for his theories about geothermal activity.

Cache Creek: One of Yellowstone's earliest named sites, this creek was named by a group of about 40 prospectors in 1864. When local Native Americans raided their camp and stole all of their horses but left two donkeys, the party cached some of their belongings here and split up, some going downstream while others went east.

Castle Geyser: This major hot spring is located in the Castle Group in the Upper Geyser Basin. Members of the Washburn expedition named this geyser in 1870 because of its strong resemblance to "an old feudal tower partially in ruins." Its interesting eruptions and its large, prominent cone have long attracted Yellowstone visitors.

Christmas Tree Park: At the turn of the 20th century, stagecoach drivers named this wooded area near West Yellowstone, Montana. The site extends eastward from the park's west boundary to near the Montana–Wyoming state line.

Christmas Tree Rock: A tradition began around 1940, when tourists at Old Faithful were stranded in one of Yellowstone's summer snowstorms. With nothing better to do, they decided to celebrate Christmas by decorating the single lodgepole pine that grows out of this rock sitting in the middle of the Firehole River. Park employees still celebrate Christmas in Yellowstone every August 25 by decorating this tree.

Cold Water Geyser: Park naturalists named Cold Water Geyser in 1954, when they made a study of its activity. The spring attracted considerable attention during the 1930s as a "cold geyser" that spouted soda water. Newspaper stories reported that people added flavoring and made sodas at the spring, which appeared to erupt to heights of 18 inches because of carbon dioxide gas.

Colter Peak: A member of the Lewis and Clark expedition, John Colter, surveyed the Yellowstone area in 1807. This 10,683-foot peak in the Absaroka Range was named by geologist Arnold Hague in 1885 to honor Colter, who was "the first white man of whom we have any record who penetrated this rough and rugged county."

Congress Pool: This hot spring in Porcelain Basin is actually named not for a political body but rather for a gathering of the Fifth International Geological Congress in Yellowstone. The pool broke out in 1891, the year that Arnold Hague and 50 other geologists congregated for the congress.

Dante's Inferno: The constantly renewing layers of sinter terraces at this site may have reminded park naturalist Al Mebane of the layers of Dante's Hell. He named this large, active, gas-driven pool in 1959.

Diamond Beach: Locals had named this long, sandy beach on Yellowstone Lake years before Captain Jones named it Crystal Beach in 1873. An early visitor to this spot had remarked that the sand "was composed almost entirely of obsidian and those minute and beautiful crystals known as California diamonds."

Dragon's Mouth Spring: This violent, seething, surging, and rumbling spring most certainly deserves its name. Over the years it has held 17 monikers—including Devil's Grotto, Devil's Workshop, and Belching Spring. In 1912, an unknown visitor christened it with this one by tacking a card to a nearby tree.

Dunraven Pass: This 8,859-foot pass in the Washburn Range bears the name of a British earl who played a large role in introducing Yellowstone to Europe. In his autobiography, Dunraven recalled eating pronghorn antelope steaks on the south slopes of Mount Washburn near this pass.

Eagle Peak: Reaching 11,358 feet, this peak is the highest in Yellowstone Park. It was named in 1885 by the members of the Hague U.S. Geological Survey party, who described the peak as "shaped like a spread eagle."

Echinus Geyser: Known as the tallest predictable geyser in the Norris area, Echinus Geyser was named by mineralogist Albert C. Peale of the Hayden survey in 1878. He took the name, which is the genus of spiny sea urchins, because "the pebbles around the basin had some resemblance to the spine-covered sea urchin."

Electric Peak: During the 1872 Hayden survey, a singular incident led to the naming of this mountain. When the survey party reached the summit of the peak during an afternoon storm, the men heard the crackling of electricity and their hair stood on end. This drove them to lower elevations.

Elephant Back Mountain: Although it had been christened by old trappers years before, this low ridge was officially named by Dr. F. V. Hayden in 1871 because "of the almost vertical sides of this mountain, and the rounded form of the summit," which resembled the back of an elephant.

Ephedra Spring: Though it was called "Little Blue Funnel Spring" in 1959, this hot spring was renamed in the 1960s for Ephedra brusei, a species of brine fly that inhabits thermal areas and feeds off hot water algae.

Fairy Falls: Tumbling 197 feet, this is the fourth-highest named waterfall in Yellowstone Park. Captain Barlow discovered it in 1871 and named it for "the graceful beauty with which the little stream dropped down a clear descent."

Falls River: This major river, which rises from large springs at the foot of Pitchstone Plateau, officially received its name in 1872 from members of the Hayden survey. Trappers had named the river much earlier, one writing in his 1838 journal of a river "which is called by hunters 'the falling fork' from the numerous cascades it forms."

Firehole River: The name of this river dates from the 1830s and is probably the park's fifth-oldest place name. It may have come from early trapper lingo suggesting a burned-over valley, or perhaps the geysers and hot springs along the river inspired the name. It appeared on maps in 1851.

Fishing Cone: What began as an early fishing accident became a huge tourist attraction for the park. A member of the 1870 Washburn party wrote of a fisherman whose catch slipped into the cone only to be boiled and suitable for eating. Well into the 1920s visitors would perform the same cooking-on-the hook feat for cameras.

Fountain Geyser: Members of the 1871 Hayden survey gave this geyser its name because of its spectacular (though unpredictable) eruptions, which usually reach 60 feet. In the early days, Fountain Geyser erupted often and became one of Yellowstone's most famous features, lending its name to a nearby hotel in 1891.

Gallatin Range: This major mountain range has gone by various names, from Upper Madison Range to Pyramid Mountains. By 1860 Mount Gallatin had appeared on maps, named for Albert Gallatin, the brilliant secretary of the treasury under Thomas Jefferson.

Gallatin River: The local Shoshone Indians originally called this branch of the Missouri River Cut-tuh-o'-gwa, which means "swift water." Lewis and Clark named the river when they reached the headwaters in 1805 in honor of Albert Gallatin, Jefferson's secretary of the treasury.

Gardner River: This river carries one of the park's oldest places names, which Johnson Gardner himself may have given to the river during the early 1830s. Gardner was a legendary fur trapper who battled with British trappers and Native Americans alike. His name, with an altered spelling, graces the town of Gardiner, Montana, as well.

Gentian Pool: First known as "Thanatopsis Spring," this pool was renamed by 1889 to reflect the blue wildflower, Gentiana thermalis, that grows nearby. Today, the blue gentian is the official flower of Yellowstone National Park.

Gibbon River: While exploring this region in 1872, members of the Hayden survey encountered a party of soldiers from Fort Ellis led by General Gibbon. The military men shared important navigational information about the river, and the survey party saw fit to assign the general's name to this major stream.

Golden Gate Canyon: Located below Rustic Falls, this canyon was probably named by workers who built the first stagecoach road in the area around 1883. The name referred to the golden color of the canyon's rock walls, caused by lichen, and to the road serving as a "gateway" into the upper park.

Grand Geyser: In recent years the Grand Geyser has been the world's tallest predictable geyser, which led to its title. With explosive eruptions rising to 200 feet in height and 6 feet in diameter, it's a favorite with park visitors.

Grand Prismatic Spring: The largest hot spring in the park and probably the third largest in the world, Grand Prismatic also has the distinction of being the earliest described Yellowstone feature. In 1839, a fur trapper reported it in his journal, describing the spring's intense colors and noting that they were reflected in the spring's vapor.

Great Fountain Geyser: One of the park's premier geysers, Great Fountain can erupt to heights of 200 feet. The Hayden survey titled this fountain in 1872 due to its "exquisite jets and columns of water, enormous in quantity."

Grotto Geyser: The intriguing topography of this geyser led the 1870

Washburn party to name the site Grotto Geyser "from its singular crater of vitrified sinter, full of large sinuous apertures." Grotto Geyser erupts up to 40 feet high in 2- to 12-hour intervals.

The Gumper: A new hot spring that developed in 1974 was named by park naturalists because of the thumping, "gumping" action of its churning mud. Some 70 feet in diameter, the Gumper claimed a bison in 1984.

Handkerchief Pool: Early visitors to the park delighted in the curious habits of this pool. It became a great attraction for visitors to put into the pool a handkerchief, which "would be sucked down and would come up in a few minutes nice and clean." By 1906, tour guides were telling visitors that this was where the devil took in washing, and by 1913 some were calling it the Devil's Laundry. It's now off-limits to approach.

Harlequin Lake: First known as Secret Lake during the 1940s, because a pair of trumpeter swans spent summers there, the lake was officially named in 1958 for the harlequin duck.

Heart Lake: An early hunter who operated in the vicinity of this lake gave his name to it before 1871. Hart Hunney operated in this region between 1840 and 1860. It's rumored that he died in a fight with Crow Indians. Later U.S. Geological Survey documents erroneously changed the spelling of the name from Hart to Heart, assuming that it referred to the shape of the lake.

Hellroaring Creek: This tributary of the Yellowstone River was given its name by a group of prospectors in 1867. Records said that one of the men left his group, "went ahead for a hunt, and upon his return he was asked what kind of stream the next creek was. 'It's a hell roarer,' was his reply, and Hellroaring is its name to this day."

Hygeia Spring: This quiet warm spring got its name in 1884 from the owners of the nearby Marchall's Hotel. Hygeia is the Greek goddess of health, and the hotel visitors used the spring's water for both bathing and culinary purposes.

Ice Box Canyon: Ice can be found until late summer on the walls of this small canyon on Soda Butte Creek. The name was used by locals at least as early as 1929.

Indian Pond: Park Superintendent P. W. Norris named this lake Indian Pond in 1880 because the local Native Americans used it for camping. Later, geologist Arnold Hague noted that the lake "appears to have been a favorite camping ground for manufacturing implements, being convenient to quarries, and nearby hunting grounds."

Iris Falls: In 1885, members of the Hague survey named this 45-foot waterfall—possibly for the Greek mythological character Iris, but most likely for its irised spray, which creates a rainbow.

Kepler Cascades: In 1881, an expedition that included young Kepler Hoyt and his father searched for a practical route into Yellowstone from Wyoming. Superintendent P. W. Norris named the falls after Kepler, "the intrepid 12-year-old son of Governor Hoyt...who unflinchingly shared all of the hardships, privations, and dangers of the explorations of his father."

Kingman Pass: On the main road between Terrace Mountain and Bunsen Peak, this pass was named for Dan Kingman of the U.S. Army Corps of Engineers. During his three years as the first road engineer in Yellowstone, he completed some 30 miles of permanent roads to "enable tourists to visit the principal points of interest in the park without retracing their steps."

Knowles Falls: This 15-foot waterfall on the Yellowstone River is named for John S. Knowles, a miner who lived in a cabin at the mouth of Crevice Creek near the falls for more than 20 years. He worked a claim and reportedly made a strike worth $40,000 before park authorities pressured him to move out.

Lamar River: One of the park's major rivers, the Lamar was named by geologist Arnold Hague in 1885. He chose the name to honor his boss, Lucius Lamar, secretary of the interior at the time, because "He has done so much for the park, and has been so good a friend that it seems only the proper thing to perpetuate his name in the park."

LeHardy's Rapids: These cascades on the Yellowstone River were named after a civilian topographer, Paul LeHardy, who was a member of the 1873 Jones expedition. He and a partner were marooned when their makeshift raft capsized at these rapids during a routine exploration of the river.

Lewis Lake: Frank Bradley of the second Hayden survey named the lake in 1872, writing: "as it had no name...we decided to call it Lewis Lake in memory of the gallant explorer Captain Lewis." In 1804–1806 Lewis and Clark passed north of Yellowstone Park by about 50 miles, so Meriwether Lewis never saw the lake.

Liberty Cap: This 37-foot-high cone of travertine from an extinct hot spring was named by F. V. Hayden in 1871. He thought it resembled the caps worn by the French during their revolution.

Lone Star Geyser: Many parties claim to have named this major geyser five miles upstream from Old Faithful. The most reliable account is in the 1874 journal of park visitor Joseph Cochran: "I took with me a board off a cracker box and nailed it up on a tree and printed on it the name 'Lone Star Geyser.'"

Lost Creek: This stream has borne many names during Yellowstone history. First known as Meadow Brook in 1871, Meadow Creek in 1872, and Strawberry Brook in 1877, it received its current name in 1878 from geologist William Holmes because "it apparently sinks from sight in the lower part of its course."

Lower Falls of the Yellowstone River: This 308-foot waterfall on the Yellowstone River is the highest in the park. Earliest recorded observations of the falls, by an early trapper in the region, date to 1826. Among many compliments the falls have evoked, the 1870 Washburn expedition wrote, "A grander scene than the lower cataract of the Yellowstone was never witnessed by mortal eyes."

Madison River: Rated the second-best trout stream in all of Yellowstone, this river, which begins at Madison Lake, was named by Lewis and Clark in 1805 "after James Madison, secretary of state."

Mammoth Hot Springs: These famous travertine hot springs attracted visitors as early as 1830. An enterprising businessman named Horr built some bathhouses on the spot to serve as a crude spa. Twenty years later, while trying to recover some money for his original "improvements," which the government had confiscated, Horr wrote, "I gave the springs the name they now bear."

Medusa Spring: In 1887, members of the Hague parties of the U.S. Geological Survey named this spring. Perhaps the shape of the spring with its numerous runoff channels reminded them of a medusa jellyfish; or the spring may have been named for the beautiful maiden in Greek mythology who was turned into a monster with snakes for hair.

Midway Geyser Basin: This group of hot springs had been named the Half-way Group in 1871 because it was between Lower and Upper Geyser Basins; the current name was applied at a later date. In previous years, the region was called by many different monikers, including Egeria Springs, Excelsior Geyser Basin, and, most famously, Hell's Half Acre.

Minerva Terrace and Minerva Spring: Named after the Roman goddess of artists and sculptors, this spring, which creates the terrace, may have been named by several people. The first record of the current name dates from 1884, when park tour guide G. L. Henderson referred to the spring as Fountain of Minerva.

Monument Geyser Basin: This region is considered one of the most curious spots in Yellowstone, with strangely formed sinter cones like gravestones or resembling "a crouching lioness...a slender chimney...a headless man." Park Superintendent P. W. Norris discovered and named this area in 1878.

Moran Point: This viewpoint on the north rim of the Grand Canyon of the Yellowstone was named for the artist Thomas Moran by members of the first Hayden survey. Moran's beautiful watercolor landscapes of the region helped to convince a skeptical Congress to establish Yellowstone as the first national park.

Morning Falls: This waterfall located in the southwestern corner of the park was named by guidebook writer Thomas B. Carter in 1976. He suggested the name because the cascade faces east and catches the rays of the morning sun.

Morning Glory Pool: The namesake spring of the Morning Glory Group is one of Yellowstone's most famous hot springs. An early tent-hotel owner may have named the spring in 1883 for its blue water, deep throat and symmetrical chalice, which resemble the morning glory flower.

Mount Everts: This high plateau was named by explorer H. D. Washburn in 1871 to honor Truman Everts, a member of his 1870 expedition who was lost in the snowy Yellowstone wilderness for 37 days. Everts survived by eating thistles boiled in geysers. When he was finally rescued he was so ungrateful that he refused to pay the rewards that had been offered!

Mount Washburn: The main peak of the Washburn Range rises 10,243 feet and is probably Yellowstone's best-known mountain. Members of the 1870 Washburn expedition unanimously named this peak for their leader after he made the first recorded climb of the mountain.

Mud Volcano: One of the park's most famous mud hot springs, this site was named by members of the Washburn party in 1870 because it was shaped like a cone volcano. Over the years, violent natural eruptions have changed the spring to a flatter and less conical shape.

Obsidian Cliff: This "mountain of glass, composed of a hard, glass-like volcanic rock called obsidian" is considered the largest deposit of this unusual rock in North America. The site was an important quarry for local Native Americans, who used the material to create arrowheads, knives, and scrapers.

Opalescent Pool: Known in the 1920s as Cerulean Spring and later as Algal Pool, this site was inadvertently named years later. In 1957, naturalist Herbert Lystrup noted that the spring "revealed an opalescent azure as the sky above" and thus the pool was renamed.

Osprey Falls: These 150-foot falls on the Gardner River were known by a variety of names, including Gardiner's Falls and Gardiner's River Falls. In 1885, members of the Hague parties named the cascades after the fish hawk, which ranges in Yellowstone territory.

Ouzel Falls: In 1885, members of the Hague parties named this 230-foot waterfall on Ouzel Creek. Yellowstone's third-highest waterfall, it was named for the water ouzel or American dipper, a small slate-colored bird that feeds underwater by diving and walking along the bottoms of streams.

Pearl Geyser: Mineralogist A. C. Peale of the Hayden survey named this erratic geyser in 1878, referring to the semitransparent geyserite "pearls" in the deposits that surround the spring.

Pelican Creek: A splinter party of the James Stuart prospecting expedition named Pelican Creek in 1864. Members' logbooks note, "We camped on this creek, and noticed several large bids which appeared to be wild geese."

Pitchstone Plateau: This vast, arid, untimbered plateau was named in

1878 by members of the third Hayden party. The plateau is composed mainly of pitchstone, a kind of obsidian and one of Yellowstone's more common volcanic rocks.

Poison Spring: Only recently called Poison Spring, this hot spring has been described as a natural gaseous deathtrap that has killed 78 birds in six weeks! The 1885 park tour operator G. L. Henderson warned visitors that this spring "must be approached with caution, keeping on the wind side on account of its poisonous gases."

Porcelain Basin: This area was first named Porcelain Vale in 1881 because of the gray-white porcelain-like geyserite formations that cover most of the basin.

Roaring Mountain: This mountainside of steaming fumaroles was named for its noisy temperament. Arnold Hague of the U.S. Geological Survey noted in 1885, "It takes its name from the shrill, penetrating sound of the steam constantly escaping from one or more vents located near the summit."

Rock Creek: Army scouts and old mountaineers named this stream as early as 1896 for Richard W. Rock, a hunter and poacher who lived in the region in the early days of the park. He is mainly remembered for his sometimes illegal efforts to capture and protect wild animals from the park.

Sheepeater Cliffs: P. W. Norris traveled through these canyons in 1879 and attached the name in honor of the Sheepeater Indian tribe, also known as the Tukudikas, the only American Indians known to live within the boundaries of the park. They were called the Sheepeaters because their staple food was bighorn sheep.

Shoshone Lake: By the time the 1872 Hayden expedition attached the current name to Yellowstone's second-largest lake, it had already borne four or five names. Noting that the lake belonged to the Snake River drainage, the Hayden party "therefore called it Shoshone Lake, adopting the Indian name of the Snake River."

Shoshone Point: This outlook was named in 1891 because Shoshone Lake could be seen from it. The point was the scene of a stagecoach holdup in 1914, in which a lone bandit stole over $1,000 in cash and jewelry from 82 passengers in a long line of vehicles.

Silver Cord Cascade: Two members of the 1870 Washburn expedition found this cascade on Surface Creek and wrote in their journal: "discovered and named falls opposite side of Yellowstone River—Silverthread fall. They pitch and plunge down the side of a canyon over 1500 feet." Actually, their estimate was high; the canyon at this point is 1,200 feet deep.

Slough Creek: This excellent cutthroat trout stream was named by prospectors in 1867. When a scout from a party of five men returned from surveying the territory up ahead, he was reported to have said of the stream "'Twas but a slough."

Snake River: The name of this mighty tributary of the Columbia River comes from the Shoshone Indians, who were also known as the Snake Indians as early as 1812. The Shoshone referred to some parts of the stream as Yampapah meaning "stream where the Yampa grows." Yampa was a staple food plant for the Shoshone.

Soda Butte Canyon: This canyon takes its name from the valley of Soda Butte Creek. The name was in use as early as 1877 by General Howard, when his military force passed through the area in pursuit of the Nez Perce Indians.

Solitary Geyser: In 1872, topographer Gustavus Bechler of the second Hayden survey included Solitary Spring on his map and thus named the spring. The geyser was heavily manipulated in the first half of the 20th century to serve as a hot water source for a swimming pool built at Old Faithful.

Specimen Ridge: The name of this long ridge was in use prior to 1870 and was probably given by prospectors. Captain Jones described the ridge in 1873 as "a noted locality for amethysts, forms of chalcedony, opal and silicified wood."

Steady Geyser: This geyser, located in the Firehole Lake Group, earned its name because it is a perpetual spouter, perhaps the world's largest, and erupts constantly. Steady Geyser has two vents that alternate between eruptive and dormant periods. First one vent shows steady action and then the other, followed by a longer period when both vents play in concert.

Steamboat Geyser: The 1878 Hayden party named this geyser because "the eruptions reminded one of the sound of an old style paddle wheel steamboat." The geyser was most active between 1888 and 1911; in those years its eruptions reached heights 100–350 feet.

Steamboat Point: This point on the northeastern shore of Yellowstone Lake was known as Steam Point, Steamboat Point, and Steamy Point by members of the Hayden party. Mineralogist Albert Peale wrote that the point was named because "of a powerful steam vent from which a vast column of steam escapes with a continuous roar."

Stygian Caves: These caves filled with poisonous gases led tour operator G. L. Henderson to name them after the River Styx in Greek mythology. The legendary Styx surrounded the underworld and was a place "from whence no traveler returns." Though the gases occasionally caused problems for human visitors, they were especially lethal to smaller animals, including birds.

Sulphur Cauldron: Some have called this the most acidic spring in the park; it has a pH of 1.3.

Terrace Mountain: Members of the third Hayden survey in 1878 named this flat plateau located above the hoodoos. Like the Mammoth terraces, Terrace Mountain is believed to have been formed by ancient hot spring activity, which deposited its travertine limestone terraces.

Uncle Tom's Point: This name seems to have come into local use from nearby Uncle Tom's Trail. "Uncle" Tom Richardson took tourists across the Yellowstone River on this trail for five years before the government revoked his permit in 1903.

Undine Falls: This double waterfall was given its name in 1885 by geologist Arnold Hague, referring to mythological water nymphs. In folklore, undines were wise, usually female, water spirits that lived in and around waterfalls.

Union Falls: This 250-foot waterfall on Mountain Ash Creek was named by members of the U.S. Geological Survey in 1884. A geologist in the group explained the reason for the name: "the water descends over rocks to 50 feet below the crest where the branch stream joins the falls. Hence 'Union Falls.'"

Upper Falls of the Yellowstone River: This 109-foot waterfall on the Yellowstone River was probably the site of many unrecorded visits by fur trappers. Members of the 1869 Folsom party were the first to refer to the falls as "upper falls" and they observed that the water went "rushing through a chute sixty feet wide, falling in an unbroken sheet."

Wahhi Falls: This 28-foot waterfall was named Two Step Falls by explorer W. C. Gregg in 1921. The U.S. Board on Geographic Names approved the name Wahhi Falls in 1922; it comes from a Shoshone word, wahat hwa, meaning "two step" or "double."

Washburn Range: This is one of only two mountain ranges entirely within the boundaries of Yellowstone Park. The Washburn party of 1870 named the main mountain after their leader, and the subsequent Hayden surveys attached the name to the entire range.

West Thumb of Yellowstone Lake: Members of the 1870 Washburn party noted that Yellowstone Lake was shaped like "a human hand with the fingers extended and spread apart as much as possible." The large west bay represented the thumb in this configuration and was given that name.

Yancey Creek: This creek was named for "Uncle" John Yancey, colorful proprietor of the Pleasant Valley Hotel, which was also known as Yancey's. The five-room hotel was said to accommodate 20 guests for $2 per day including meals, and it was situated near the mouth of Yancey Creek.

Yellowstone River: This is the oldest place name in the park. The colorful name has debatable origins, but a 1981 Crow chief asserted that the name came about as a mistake in translation. "In our language we always called it the Elk River. The words sound alike, and the French didn't understand Crow very well."

PRESERVATION ORGANIZATIONS AND PROJECTS

Yellowstone National Park is challenged by increasing development along its borders and increasing visitation within its borders. To help ensure that it remains wild and unimpaired for the future, two organizations have been established. The Yellowstone Association and the Yellowstone Park Foundation work in partnership with the National Park Service and each other to provide opportunities for visitors to contribute to Yellowstone's preservation. A third organization, the Greater Yellowstone Coalition, is dedicated to protecting the resources and wildlands of the Greater Yellowstone Area, including Yellowstone National Park. Here's a description of some of the projects that these three organizations are engaged in, and how you can help each of them to preserve Yellowstone for future generations.

Yellowstone Association

The Yellowstone Association (P.O. Box 117, Yellowstone National Park, WY 82190, 307/344-2293, www.yellowstoneassociation.org) is a nonprofit educational organization founded in 1933 to aid historical, scientific, and educational programs for the benefit of Yellowstone National Park and its visitors. Among many past and present activities, the association:

- operates bookstores in visitor centers throughout the park, with proceeds going to support park programs
- founded the Yellowstone Association Institute in 1976, which offers educational courses for all ages
- publishes booklets for self-guided trail tours of thermal areas
- publishes books and pamphlets pertaining to Yellowstone National Park
- assists naturalists with visitor information services at visitor centers
- administers grants and gifts for designated projects in Yellowstone
- helps fund seasonal training for park naturalists
- contributes annual funds for park exhibits, educational programs, and research projects
- provides continued support to Yellowstone's research library through purchase of materials and employment of staff.

Contact the Yellowstone Association to become a member. Along with the pleasure of knowing that you're directly supporting the park's preservation, members receive benefits such as subscriptions to the park newspaper and member magazine; a 15 percent discount at Yellowstone Association's park stores and online store, discounts at Yellowstone Institute classes, and more.

Yellowstone Park Foundation

The Yellowstone Park Foundation (222 E. Main St., Ste. 301, Bozeman, MT 59715, 406/586-6303, www.ypf.org) is a nonprofit organization created by a group of concerned citizens, working with the National Park Service, to preserve, protect, and enhance Yellowstone National Park and to enrich each visitor's experience. The park can no longer depend solely on federal appropriations, which lag behind the park's growing needs each year. The foundation funds important projects and programs in support of the park including:

• A bison exhibit and interpretive display that chronicles the unique history and ecological role of bison in Yellowstone

• A Fort Yellowstone self-guiding trail, where visitors learn about the vital role of the U.S. army in the park's rich history

• A landmark project to restore the park's native west-slope cutthroat trout population.

The foundation receives no government funding; it relies solely on the support of private citizens, foundations, and corporations to ensure that Yellowstone is preserved with its beauty intact for future generations. Contact the foundation to become a Friend of Yellowstone.

Greater Yellowstone Coalition

The Greater Yellowstone Coalition (P.O. Box 1874, Bozeman, MT 59771, 406/586-1593, www.greateryellowstone.org) is a nonprofit conservation organization founded in 1983 to preserve and protect the spectacular wildlands and resources of the Greater Yellowstone Ecosystem. Some of its conservation projects include:

• Working with park officials to protect park resources, manage visitation, and ensure that wildlife can migrate onto surrounding public lands

• Using educational materials, research, and community assistance to help farmers and ranchers stay on the land and to protect key habitats

• Working with other conservation groups to protect critical grizzly bear habitat

• Working with irrigators, ranchers, and other groups at the watershed level to protect aquatic resources and restore important cold-water fisheries

• Helping to negotiate an agreement to stop a massive gold mine operation on the border of Yellowstone, which would have been detrimental to the park and surrounding wildlands and rivers

- Contact the coalition to join.

Recycling in Yellowstone

In 1990, Yellowstone National Park instituted a parkwide recycling program for aluminum cans, glass, and some paper products, which it hopes to expand in the coming years. Park visitors are encouraged to deposit aluminum cans and glass in special receptacles, located in all developed areas and campgrounds. Xanterra Parks & Resorts has also implemented a recycling program in Yellowstone that recycles 230 tons of material each year.

TELEPHONE AND WEBSITE DIRECTORY

GENERAL INFORMATION

Delaware North Parks and Resorts www.visityellowstonepark.com	406/586-7593
National Park Service www.nps.gov/yell	307/344-7381
Xanterra Parks & Resorts www.travelyellowstone.com	307/344-7311 or 866/439-7375 (reservations)
Yellowstone Association www.YellowstoneAssociation.org	307/344-2293

GETTING THERE

Educational fee waivers	307/344-2107
Gray Line Bus Tours www.grayline.com	800/443-6133
Greater Yellowstone Coalition www.greateryellowstone.org.	406/586-1593 or 800/775-1834
Greater Yellowstone Coordinating Committee http://bsi.montana.edu/web/gycc/home	406/522-8575
Greyhound Bus Lines www.greyhound.com	800/231-2222
Road conditions	307/344-7381
Yellowstone Park Service Stations www.nps.gov/yell/planyourvisit/gasstatn.htm	406/848-7333
Yellowstone Park Medical Services	307/344-7965
Yellowstone Today www.nps.gov/yell/planyourvisit/yellowstone-today.htm	

KENNELS

All West Veterinary Hospital	406/586-4919
Bozeman Veterinary Hospital	406/587-4275
Cody Veterinary Hospital	307/587-3151
Colmey Pet Plaza	406/222-1440

Critter Sitter	307/733-1407
Dog on Wheels	406/763-4214
Gallatin Veterinary Hospital	406/587-4458
Jackson Hole	307/733-4279
Kennels West	406/587-7446
Kindness Kennels	307/733-2633
Livingston Veterinary Hospital	406/222-3011
Pet Set	307/587-9515
Spring Creek Kennels	307/733-1606
Valley View Veterinary Boarding	406/586-9094

PARK ATTRACTIONS

Albright Visitor Center	307/344-2263
Canyon Visitor Education Center	307/344-2550
Colter Bay Visitor Center	307/739-3594
Fishing Bridge Visitor Center	307/242-2450
Gallatin National Forest Ranger Station	406/848-7375 or 406/848-7376
Grant Village Visitor Center	307/242-2650
National Park Service Public Affairs Office	307/344-2013
Old Faithful Visitor Center	307/344-2750
Xanterra Parks & Resorts www.travelyellowstone.com	307/344-7311 or 866/439-7375

GETTING AROUND

Gray Line Bus Tours www.grayline.com	800/443-6133
Jack Dennis Fishing Trips www.jackdennis.com	307/733-3270
Jackson Hole Kayak School www.jacksonholekayak.com	307/733-2471
John Henry Lee Outfitters www.johnhenrylee.com	307/455-3200 or 800/352-2576
Taylor Outfitters metaylor@wyoming.com	307/455-2161

Ranger-led programs
www.nps.gov/yell

| Road conditions | 307/344-7381 |
| www.nps.gov/yell/planyourvisit/hours.htm | |

| Xanterra Parks & Resorts | 307/344-7311 or 866/439-7375 |
| www.travelyellowstone.com | |

| Westbank Anglers | 307/733-6483 or 800/922-3474 |
| www.westbank.com | |

| Yellowstone Association Institute | 307/344-2293 |
| www.yellowstoneassociation.org | |

| Yellowstone Park Service Stations | 406/848-7333 or 307/344-2132 |
| www.nps.gov/yell/planyourvisit/gasstatn.htm | |

Yellowstone Today
www.nps.gov/yell/planyourvisit/yellowstone-today.htm

LODGING AND DINING

Lodging Inside the Park

| Xanterra Parks & Resorts | 307/344-7311 or 866/439-7375 |
| www.travelyellowstone.com | |

Dining Inside the Park

General information
www.nps.gov/yell/planyourvisit/wheretoeat.htm

| Xanterra Parks & Resorts | 307/344-7311 or 866/439-7375 |
| www.travelyellowstone.com | |

Special Events

| Grand Teton Music Festival | 307/733-3050 |
| www.gtmf.org | |

| Mountain Man Rendezvous (Teton Village, WY) | 307/739-2753 |

| Old West Days (Jackson Hole, WY) | 307/733-3316 |

| Stampede Days (Cody, Wyoming) | 307/587-2297 |

| Yellowstone Ski Festival (West Yellowstone, MT) | 406/646-7701 |
| www.yellowstoneskifestival.com | |

| Yellowstone Rendezvous Race (West Yellowstone, MT) | 406/646-7701 |
| www.rendezvousrace.com | |

CAMPING AND BACKPACKING

Backcountry outfitters
www.nps.gov/yell/planyourvisit/stockbusn.htm

Bridge Bay Marina	307/242-3880
Buffalo Ranger District/Blackrock Ranger Station (Bridger-Teton National Forest)	307/543-2386
Colter Bay Campground (Grand Teton National Park)	800/628-9988
Flagg Ranch Resort and Campground (2 mi. south of S. Entrance) www.flaggranch.com	800/443-2311
Gardiner Ranger District (Gallatin National Forest)	406/848-7375
Grand Teton National Park	307/739-3603
Hebgen Lake Ranger District (Gallatin National Forest)	406/823-6961
Island Park Ranger District (Targhee National Forest)	208/558-7301
Madison Arm Resort (10 mi. north of West Yellowstone) www.madisonarmresort.com	406/646-9328
National forest campgrounds www.recreation.gov	877/444-6777
National Park Service www.nps.gov/yell/planyourvisit/camping-in-yellowstone.htm	307/344-7381
North Zone Ranger District (Shoshone National Forest)	307/527-6921
Rocky Mountain Campground (Gardiner, MT)	877/534-6931
Xanterra Parks & Resorts www.travelyellowstone.com	307/344-7311 or 866/439-7375
Yellowstone Association Institute www.yellowstoneassociation.org	307/344-2293
Yellowstone Central Backcountry Office www.nps.gov/yell/planyourvisit/backcountryhiking.htm	307/344-2160 or 307/344-2163
Yellowstone Grizzly RV Park (West Yellowstone, MT) www.grizzlyrv.com	406/646-4466
Yellowstone Park www.yellowstonepark.com/PlanYourTrip/CampingInfo.aspx	

RECREATIONAL OPPORTUNITIES

Albright Visitor Center	307/344-2263
Bicycle outfitting companies www.nps.gov/yell/planyourvisit/bikebusn.htm	
Bicycling www.nps.gov/yell/planyourvisit/bicycling.htm	
Boating www.nps.gov/yell/planyourvisit/boating.htm	
Boat trip outfitters www.nps.gov/yell/planyourvisit/boatbusn.htm	
Bridge Bay Backcountry Office	307/242-2413
Bridge Bay Marina	307/242-3880
Chief Ranger's Office	307/344-2105
Fishing outfitters www.nps.gov/yell/planyourvisit/fishbsn.htm	
Fishing regulations www.nps.gov/yell/planyourvisit/fishing.htm	
Horseback riding www.nps.gov/yell/planyourvisit/horseride.htm	
Horse pack trips www.nps.gov/yell/planyourvisit/stockbusn.htm	
Old Faithful Visitor Center	307/545-2750
Road conditions	307/344-7381
Skiing information www.yellowstonenationalpark.com/skiing.htm	
Ski shops	307/344-7311, 307/344-5276 Mammoth, 307/545-4825 Old Faithful
Winter outfitters www.nps.gov/yell/planyourvisit/wintbusn.htm	
Xanterra Parks & Resorts www.travelyellowstone.com	307/344-7311 or 866/439-7375
Yellowstone Association Institute www.yellowstoneassociation.org	307/344-2293
Yellowstone Central Backcountry Office www.nps.gov/yell/planyourvisit/backcountryhiking.htm	307/344-2160 or 307/344-2163

EDUCATIONAL PROGRAMS AND FACILITIES

Buffalo Bill Historical Center	307/587-4771
Museum of the Mountain Man	307/367-4101
Museum of the National Park Ranger	307/344-7353
Museum of the Rockies	406/994-2251
National Bighorn Sheep Interpretive Center	307/455-3429
National Wildlife Art Museum	307/733-5771
Norris Geyser Basin Museum	307/344-2812
Teton Science School www.tetonscience.org	307/733-4765
Xanterra Parks & Resorts www.travelyellowstone.com	307/344-7311 or 866/439-7375
Yellowstone Association Institute www.yellowstoneassociation.org	307/344-2293

FAMILY ATTRACTIONS

Old Faithful Visitor Center	307/545-2750
Xanterra Parks & Resorts www.travelyellowstone.com	307/344-7311 or 866/439-7375
The Yellowstone Association www.yellowstoneassociation.org	307/344-2293

PRESERVATION ORGANIZATIONS AND PROJECTS

Greater Yellowstone Coalition www.greateryellowstone.org	406/586-1593
The Yellowstone Association www.yellowstoneassociation.org	307/344-2293
Yellowstone Park Foundation www.ypf.org	406/586-6303

WHERE CAN WE FIND...?

Lake Hospital	307/242-7241
Lost and found	307/344-2107
Mammoth Hot Springs Clinic	307/344-7965

National Parks passes http://store.usgs.gov/pass	888/275-8747 ext. 1
Old Faithful Clinic	307/344-7965
Park ranger assistance	307/344-2132
Park Volunteer Office	307/344-2039
Services for visitors with disabilities	307/344-2019
Xanterra Human Resources www.yellowstonejobs.com	307/344-5324
The Yellowstone Association www.yellowstoneassociation.org	307/344-2293
Yellowstone Center for Resources	307/344-2203
Yellowstone General Stores employment www.visityellowstonepark.com	
Yellowstone Park Service Stations	406/848-7333 or 307/344-2132

WHERE CAN WE FIND...?

Where Can We Find a Gas Station?

The Yellowstone Park Service Stations (406/848-7333 or 307/344-2132) company operates seven full-service gas stations: two in the Old Faithful area and one each at Grant Village, Fishing Bridge, Canyon Village, Tower Junction, and Mammoth Hot Springs. All gas, auto accessories, and oil are available only May–October. Snowmobile fuel is available during the winter at Old Faithful, Fishing Bridge, Canyon Village, and Mammoth Hot Springs.

Where Can We Find an Auto Towing and Repair Service?

The Yellowstone Park Service Stations (406/848-7333 or 307/344-2132) company operates four auto towing and repair shops in the park: at Old Faithful, Grant Village, Fishing Bridge, and Canyon Village. Repairs and routine maintenance are available only May–October.

Where Can We Buy Propane or Diesel Fuel?

You can purchase propane fuel at the Old Faithful, Grant Village, and Fishing Bridge service stations, run by Yellowstone Park Service Stations (406/848-7333 or 307/344-2132), May–October. Diesel fuel is available at those stations and the Mammoth Hot Springs station.

Where Can We Find Public Restrooms? A Public Shower? A Public Laundromat?

Public restrooms are located at all visitor centers and inside all lodging facilities throughout the park. Nonflush toilets are located along the 370 miles of paved roadways throughout the park. Public showers and laundries are at Grant Village Campground, Fishing Bridge RV Park, Canyon Village Campground, Mammoth Hot Springs, and the Old Faithful area. Lake Lodge has public laundry facilities, and Old Faithful Lodge has public showers only. Most facilities are closed during the winter.

Where Can We Find a Post Office?

The main post office, located in a historic 1930s building at Mammoth Hot Springs, is open all year. During the summer months, post office facilities are also available at Old Faithful, Lake Village, Canyon Village, and Grant Village.

Where Can We Find a Bank?

ATMs are located at Old Faithful Inn, Lake Hotel, and Canyon Lodge. There are banks in the gateway communities of Gardiner and West Yellowstone, Montana, and Cody and Jackson, Wyoming.

Where Can We Cash a Check or Exchange Foreign Currency?
You can exchange foreign currency and cash checks, if you're a hotel guest, at the front desk of any park lodge Monday–Friday 8 A.M.–5 P.M. There's a limit of $50 per day.

Where Is the Lost and Found?
You can turn in or trace lost and found articles at any visitor center or ranger station. Call 307/344-2107, or write to Yellowstone National Park, Visitor Services Office, P.O. Box 168, Yellowstone, WY 82190.

Where Can We Receive Medical Services?
Dial 911 for emergency fire, medical, or ranger assistance or to report accidents or injuries. To contact a park ranger, call 307/344-2132. National Park Service emergency medical technicians and park medics are on duty 24 hours a day year-round. In addition, there are three patient-care facilities in the park: the Mammoth Hot Springs Clinic (307/344-7965, year-round), the Old Faithful Clinic (307/344-7965, seasonally), and the Lake Hospital (307/242-7241, seasonally).

Where Can We Use a Photocopy or Fax Machine?
Old Faithful Inn, Lake Yellowstone Hotel, and Mammoth Hot Springs Hotel have photocopy and fax machines at their front desks, which the public can use. You can also send or receive a fax at the main post office in Mammoth Hot Springs.

Where Can We Get an America the Beautiful Pass?
America the Beautiful—National Parks and Federal Recreational Lands Passes (good for all national parks for one year from the date of purchase) replaces the Golden Eagle Passport, National Parks Pass, and Golden Eagle Hologram pass. It can be purchased from rangers at park entrance stations, by phone (888/ASK-USGS ext. 1), or online (http://store.usgs.gov/pass). The cost is $80 annually. Golden Age Passes, which are lifetime passes to all national parks, have been replaced by the America the Beautiful—Senior Pass, which can also only be purchased at the same locations and require a one-time $10 fee when issued to qualifying senior citizens (U.S. citizens or legal residents age 62 or older).

Where Can We Find Out About Getting a Job in Yellowstone?

Xanterra Parks & Resorts hires seasonal employees to live and work in Yellowstone. A wide variety of positions is available to eligible candidates. Contact Xanterra Human Resources (307/344-5324, www.yellowstonejobs. com). Every year, Yellowstone General Stores hires seasonal staff to work in its 14 general stores and photo shops throughout the park. For more information or an employment application, visit the Delaware North Parks and Resorts website (www.visityellowstonepark.com).

Where Can We Learn About Volunteering in the Park?

Ways to volunteer in Yellowstone abound. Call the park's Volunteer Office at 307/344-2039 for more information on volunteering in wildlife, resources, and archaeological programs, among others.

Where Is the Yellowstone Association Institute Office?

During the summer, the Yellowstone Association Institute (307/344-2293, www.yellowstoneassociation.org) is headquartered at the historic Lamar Buffalo Ranch in the Lamar Valley. Follow the Northeast Entrance Road (Hwy. 89) from Tower Junction toward the Cooke City entrance. The ranch overlooks the Lamar Valley on the north side of the road.

Where Is the Yellowstone Association Office?

The YA (307/344-2293, www.yellowstoneassociation.org) is headquartered in the Chittenden House building at Fort Yellowstone in Mammoth Hot Springs.

Where Can We Learn More About Yellowstone Resources?

The Yellowstone Center for Resources (307/344-2203) is housed in the wooden barracks building, two buildings south of the superintendent's office building. Call them first for information about park research and resource management.

Where Is the Park Superintendent's Office? The Chief Ranger's Office?

The park superintendent's and the chief ranger's offices are located in the largest building in Fort Yellowstone, the Double Cavalry Barracks building (#16 on the walking tour of Fort Yellowstone) at Mammoth Hot Springs. The building is directly behind the main post office at Mammoth.

Where Can We Find Out About Services for Disabled Visitors?

You can pick up a brochure listing facilities, scenic areas, and features accessible to visitors with disabilities at any visitor center in the park. Or you can contact the Special Populations Coordinator (Yellowstone National Park, WY 82190, 307/344-2019).

WILDERNESS CAMPERS' & BACKPACKERS' CHECKLIST

Clothes

- Sturdy hiking boots
- Thick hiking socks
- Lightweight liner socks
- Long underwear
- Fleece pants and sweatshirt
- Rain-resistant jacket and pants
- Warm hat
- Warm gloves
- Oversocks and gaiters
- Extra clothes for layering: T-shirt, long-sleeved shirt, down vest or light jacket, large bandanna
- UV-protection sunglasses

Equipment
For hiking:

- Water bottle (at least quart size)
- Topographical map
- Compass
- Pocketknife with can opener
- Watch
- Water purification device
- Flashlight or headlamp, fresh alkaline cells, and spare bulb
- Bear spray

For camping, add:

- Rain-resistant sleeping bag and pad
- Backpacking tent, fly, and stakes
- Frame backpack
- Backpacking stove and fuel
- Cooking pot, cup, and utensils

- Fire starter kit (waterproof matches in waterproof container, candle, dry paper)
- Lightweight rope for hanging food

Supplies

- Sunscreen
- Insect repellent
- Lip balm
- Small first-aid kit with blister care items
- Toilet items
- Food (including emergency rations such as raisins, nuts, hard candy)
- Extra sealable plastic bags

Further Reading

Many of the following books may be purchased from the Yellowstone Association (P.O. Box 117, Yellowstone National Park, WY 82190, 307/344-2293, www.yellowstoneassociation.org) bookstores located in visitor centers and other facilities throughout the park.

- *The Bears of Yellowstone* by Paul Schullery. Worland, Wyoming: High Plains Publishing, 1992.

- *Birds of Yellowstone* by Terry McEneaney. Boulder, Colorado: Roberts Rinehart, Inc., 1988.

- *Compass American Guides: Montana,* sixth edition, by Norma Tirrell. Oakland, California: Compass American Guides, Fodor's Travel publications, Inc., 2006.

- *Cross-Country Skiing Yellowstone Country* by Ken and Dena Olsen and Steve and Hazel Scharosch. Casper, Wyoming: Abacus Enterprises, Falcon Press, 1992.

- *Day Hiking Yellowstone* by Tom Carter. Yellowstone National Park: Thomas B. Carter, 1990.

- *Death in Yellowstone* by Lee H. Whittlesey. Boulder, Colorado: Roberts Rinehart Publishers, 1995.

- *Ecology of Jackson Hole, Wyoming: A Primer* by Tim W. Clark, Ph.D. Salt Lake City, Utah: Paragon Press, 1981.

- *Exploring Beyond Yellowstone* by Ron Adkison. Berkeley, California: Wilderness Press, 1996.

- *A Field Guide to Yellowstone's Geysers, Hot Springs and Fumaroles* by Carl Schreier. Moose, Wyoming: Homestead Publishing, 1992 (revised).

- *The Greater Yellowstone Ecosystem: Redefining America's Wilderness Heritage,* edited by Robert B. Keiter and Mark S. Boyce. New Haven, Connecticut: Yale University Press, 1991.

- *Indian Legends from the Northern Rockies* by Ella E. Clark. University of Oklahoma Press: Norman and London, 1966.

- *The Kid's Guide to Yellowstone National Park* by the students of Jackson Hole Middle School. Jackson, Wyoming: Pioneer Press, 1998.

- *Lost in the Yellowstone: Truman Evert's "Thirty-Seven Days of Peril"* edited by Lee H. Whittlesey. Salt Lake City, Utah: University of Utah Press, 1995.

- *Mountain State Mammals* by Ron Russo, Illustrated by Barbara Downs. Rochester, New York: Nature Study Guild, 1991.

- *Mountain Time: A Yellowstone Memoir* by Paul Schullery. Boulder, Colorado: Roberts Rinehart Publishers, 1995.

- *Nature's Yellowstone* by Richard A. Bartlett. Tucson, Arizona: The University of Arizona Press, 1974.

- *The Old Faithful Inn: A National Historical Landmark* by Dorothy K. Hilburn. Bellemont, Arizona: Canyonlands Publications, 1997.

- *Plants of the Rocky Mountains* by Linda Kershaw, Andy McKinnon, and Jim Pojar. Edmonton, Alberta: Lone Pine Publishing, 1998.

- *Preserving Yellowstone's Natural Conditions* by James A. Pritchard. University of Nebraska Press, 1999.

- *Searching For Yellowstone: Ecology and Wonder in the Last Wilderness* by Paul Schullery. Boston and New York: Houghton Company, 1997.

- *Waterfalls of Yellowstone National Park* by Charles Maynard. Seymour, Tennessee: Panther Press, 1996.

- *The Wolves of Yellowstone* by Michael K. Phillips and Douglas W. Smith. Stillwater, Minnesota: Voyageur Press, Inc., 1996.

- *Yellowstone Fishing Guide* by Robert E. Charlton. Ketchum, Idaho: Lost River Press, 1995.

- *Yellowstone Grand Teton Road Guide* by Jeremy Schmidt and Steven Fuller. Jackson Hole, Wyoming: Free Wheeling Guides, 1998.

- *Yellowstone: Land of Fire and Ice* by Gretel Ehrlich. New York: Tehabi Books and HarperCollins West, 1995.

- *Yellowstone National Park* by Patty Knapp. Moose, Wyoming: Children's Outdoor Library, 1997.

- *Yellowstone: The Official Guide to Touring America's First National Park* by The Yellowstone Association, Yellowstone National Park, 1997.

- *Yellowstone Place Names* by Lee H. Whittlesey. Helena, Montana: A Montana Historical Society Guide, 1988.

- *The Yellowstone Story, Volumes I and II* by Aubrey L. Haines. Yellowstone National Park: Yellowstone Association, 1996.

- *Yellowstone Trails* by Mark C. Marschall. Yellowstone National Park: Yellowstone Association, 2003.

- *Yellowstone: A Visitor's Companion* by George Wuerthner, Harrisburg, PA.: Stackpole Books, 1992.

- *Yellowstone Wolves in the Wild* by James C. Halfpenny, Helena, Montana: Riverbend Publishing, 2003.

Index

SUSAN AND PHIL FRANK

Susan Frank spent many of her childhood weekends camping in the Sierra Nevada and fishing California rivers and lakes with her family. She saw her first grizzly bear on the Katmai Peninsula in Alaska at age ten and spent more enjoyable hours waiting for fish to bite her line than actually catching them. After earning a degree in European history from the University of California, Berkeley, she taught in Minnesota and California before starting a career in communications. In 1990, she founded a media and marketing consulting company, working with a variety of clients throughout the San Francisco Bay Area.

Cartoonist Phil Frank's daily cartoon strip *Farley* kept a finger on the pulse of the San Francisco Bay Area for more than 21 years, ever since Phil decided to move the strip from national syndication to focus his considerable talents on issues closer to home. The strip was dearly loved and followed daily by a local cadre of fans. Indeed, *Farley* became one of San Francisco's most recognized and reliable landmarks. In 2004, Phil started a nationally syndicated strip with writer Joe Troise called *Elderberries*, which turned a humorous eye to the issues of aging in America. Phil passed away in September of 2007, but his *Elderberries* strip still runs in newspapers across the country.

Susan and Phil started their life together on a houseboat in Sausalito, California. This led to their first book collaboration, a children's book about living on the water. Both avid history buffs, they moved from ship to shore about 10 years ago. Susan lives in Sausalito in a 1914 Craftsman-style home, from which she ventures into California's national parks and other wilderness areas in search of inspiration for new books. Her family includes two grown children, three grandchildren, and Gus, a feisty Cairn Terrier.